Wait, How Many Pages?

The Bedrock for Conquering Capstone

Jennifer M. Gmuca

ii

Printed in the United States of America
ISBN 978-1-7368612-7-1

For my loving husband Brennen and daughters Penelope and Evangeline, this would not have been feasible without your love and support.
I love you, always!

A special thank you to my dear friend, Laura Rice, for all your help, patience, and support.

I want to acknowledge the entire Sentia Publishing team with whom I had the pleasure of working. Without you, this book would not have been possible. I am beyond grateful for this fantastic opportunity!

TABLE OF CONTENTS

INTRODUCTION

Congratulations! The time has come to begin your Capstone Seminar adventure. Many students find this course intimidating; it is normal if you feel that way too. You will be utilizing the skills you have been taught over the past three years to select a topic, write a lengthy research paper, and present your critical analysis to an audience of your peers. This handbook is designed to guide you through this process. The title of this text is derived from the reaction students have to the size of the Capstone paper. "Wait, how many pages is it?" Yes, it is a hefty 20+ page research paper that requires around 20 sources, but do not be deterred. After reading this manual, you will possess the bedrock to conquer Capstone Seminar. The following is the course description of the Capstone Seminar at Mount Aloysius College.

> "Capstone Seminar is the demonstration of the student's mastery of the undergraduate discipline and its synthesis with the liberal arts. Through the culminating research project, students demonstrate the ability to write and effectively communicate depth in the discipline, integration of liberal arts...."[1]

The text is designed with you, the student, in mind. Ideally, it will serve as a refresher and, in some cases, an instructional guide for completing the major Capstone assignments. Best of all, it is all in one place. I created this handbook after working with students in Capstone Preparatory courses. Many of my students complained about feeling unprepared for the tasks they would undertake in the final Capstone Seminar. A significant struggle that students encounter is knowing

---

[1] "LA 400-Capstone Seminar." *Mount Aloysius College* (2021). http://catalog.mtaloy.edu/preview_course_nopop.php?catoid=1&coid=366

what components go with which assignment. This guide will address the most popular writing assignments, research advice, and presentation methods.

Along with assignment components, the term reliable will be preached while conducting the research process. Students must recognize source reliability; fortunately, a section of this text is wholly devoted to the validity of sources.

This text covers the three major components of the Capstone Seminar:

- A research project culminating in a sizeable final paper
- Research methodology and literature review
- Creation and delivery of oral presentations

A capstone research project is a considerable undertaking and needs to be approached skillfully. Though it may be difficult, with proper preparation, students can enjoy the entire process. So often students are required to write on topics that they did not choose. In Capstone, you will be selecting a paper topic based on your primary discipline.

To complete the research projects, students must do just that—research. Researching goes beyond locating articles, books, and websites. You must understand the best research methodology for the topic of choice and the reliability of the selected scholarship. There is that word again-reliable. Be prepared to hear that word until you are sick of it. Your instructors are not saying it repeatedly to be annoying. It is a critical aspect of producing an academic paper.

To conclude, students will be presenting their findings to their peers. This presentation is accomplished with a multimedia presentation, a poster board presentation, or a lecture. The best way to diminish speech anxiety is proper preparation, and this text will help you become prepared.

CHAPTER 1: MAJOR PAPER

As you reach the end of your academic career, it is essential to reflect on the information you learned. You have dedicated years of your life to studying a particular field in the hopes of advancing into the ideal career. Think of Capstone Seminar as your opportunity to showcase your new finely tuned talents acquired during your tenure. As the University of Virginia's Capstone webpage states, "We don't care where you start; we care where you finish."[2]

During Capstone Seminar, you will utilize the research skills you acquired through higher education to write an extensive research paper. The primary paper will demand various skills, such as research, writing, analysis, and critical thinking. You will accomplish this task through guided independent research, where you will select a topic relevant to your field. The term guided independent research means that you, the student, will have deadlines for assignments, but you will be working independently to meet deadlines. *Wait How Many Pages?* is designed to make this research project more obtainable as it condenses popular writing assignments into one location.

Onward, the topic you select should be of particular interest to you, since you will be spending much time researching and analyzing crucial scholarship. Admittedly, student success correlates to the student's interest in the unique subject. Throughout the capstone research project,

---

[2] "Capstone – BIS," *School of Continuing and Professional Studies: The University of Virginia,* accessed September 9, 2021, https://www.scps.virginia.edu/bachelor-of-liberal-arts/capstone

students are expected to demonstrate depth and understanding of their discipline. Additionally, research will help you reach a deep understanding of the topic at hand.

The term capstone will be repetitive throughout this text. It is essential to understand the meaning of this term to understand the nature of your project. Let us begin with a brief history of the term. The etymology of the word capstone derives from a cap-stone that is used to complete a building or a monument—literally meaning the final stone in the architectural project. The term capstone has a similar meaning in higher education as the course and corresponding projects translate into the finishing piece of your education—the final stone. This capstone course will demonstrate all the skills or building blocks you have acquired while studying your designated field. These skills will be demonstrated in a "capstone project [,] meaning… an academic research study of a student, carried out in the final phase of education. Performing the project within the curriculum is the highest level of student research, encouraging future professionals to search for creativity."[3]

While capstone projects vary from school to school, the course is generally designed to illustrate that you, the student, have gained a strong bedrock of knowledge in your field. It will further show that while it is impossible to know everything about your potential career path, you can confidently acknowledge ignorance, knowing you have the skills to find the correct answer. In other words, "I don't know, but I can research to find out."

This simple phrase is often underestimated by those who utter it. Never underestimate the power to acknowledge ignorance while simultaneously exuding confidence in the ability to learn.

---

[3] "What is a Capstone Project at School, College, or University," *Capstone Writing*, accessed September 9, 2021, https://capstonewriting.com/blog/what-is-capstone-project-definition/

It speaks volumes about your intellectual abilities. Likewise, the prowess required to complete a large, challenging research project will give you the confidence necessary to enter a career with a ferocity to excel. So, approach this course with a solid fervor to illustrate the exceptionally fine-tuned skills you must learn throughout the college experience.

1.1 Knowing the Citation Style of Your Field

It is essential to understand that you will use the citation style corresponding with your field's discipline. So even though, you and your roommate were lucky enough to take the same section of Capstone Seminar, that does not mean you will be writing in the same citation style. Since different disciplines follow a different format, you will be required to use the citation style of your individual major.

This raises the question of what citation style do you belong to? Do not be embarrassed if you have made it this far in college and are still confused about the citation style that corresponds with your major! I assure you; you are not alone. To overcome this hurdle, let us explore the citation styles plus the discipline to which they belong. If you are still unsure of your major's citation style after reading this, ask your instructor for help. We are here to help you, after all.

Usually, the recognized citation styles can be located on the school's library webpage under LibGuides. Most, if not all, institutions in higher education have LibGuides available to their students.

The three most widely used styles of citation are APA, MLA, and Chicago (Turabian). According to the Mount Aloysius College's LibGuide, the following authority corresponds with the noted disciplines:

- **APA** — the American Psychological Association.
  - o Use for Social Sciences, such as Psychology, Linguistics, Sociology, Economics, Criminology, Fine Arts, Art History, and Business.

- **MLA** — the Modern Language Association.
  - o Use for English Studies, including Language and Literature, Foreign Languages and Literature, Literary Criticism, Comparative Literature, and Cultural Studies.

- **Chicago Style** — the Chicago Manual of style.
  - o Use for History and Political Science.[4]
  - o Note that Chicago can also be abbreviated CMOS or CMS. If you hear the term Turabian, please note that it is nearly identical to Chicago which is slightly simplified to help students understand it better.[5]

---

[4] "Citation Style Guides: Home," *LibGuides Mount Aloysius College,* March 30, 2021, https://libguides.mtaloy.edu/citation_style_guides. Note that I have not listed the editions. It is your responsibility to look up the current version of the citation style since the versions are often updated and changing.

[5] Ibid.

The above definitions should help you identify the manual of style you belong to based on your major. But, do you understand how and when to use it? A citation style dictates everything from the font size, margin spacing, heading, and subheads to the list of sources. Always cite anything that is not your original thought. To learn more about the recommended texts for your citation style, ask your professor. Citation format and style must be implemented into all the assignments in Capstone Seminar. It is not recommended that you use citation generators because the programs format citations incorrectly. So, please take the time to create your bibliographic entry.

CHAPTER 2: PRE-WRITING

The art of pre-writing provides the writer with an opportunity to clarify and organize ideas. Commonly, students struggle to narrow or broaden their topics to something that is obtainable within the parameters of the assignment instructions. Through the use of drafting, you can help clarify your ideas into something that is manageable.

Within this section, you will find the most popular assignments which make up the writing portion of the Capstone project. While this is an extensive list, it is essential to note that it is not exhaustive. Professors have the power to change anything about the following assignments—task the assignments in a different order, omit a few, or add a project not covered. You must pay close attention to the syllabus, instructions, and rubric before you begin any assignment in Capstone. The purpose of this guide is for you to be as prepared and informed as possible by covering a variety of traditional research-intensive writing assignments.

Featured in this chapter are directions for a topic proposal, which is a relatively simple assignment, and it informs the instructor of your intended search topic. The elements of a research proposal are addressed. Pay close attention to this assignment. Many of you will write proposals throughout your career; while the proposal may look different in a business setting, it embodies the same goals. Another assignment herein is the research prospectus. This multi-part project will force you to become aware of problems you may encounter throughout the research and writing process.

2.1 Topic Proposal

The first step to designing a research project is getting your mind right. The student must approach the course and corresponding assignments with the proper state of mind. If you look at a research paper as an imposition, something you must do to graduate, then you are more likely to struggle. On the contrary, students who approach it with a positive mindset considering it one last step to conclude the undergraduate experience and an opportunity to showcase the skills acquired during tenure, are more likely to have a good experience. State of mind is critical to having a positive experience with a positive outcome, not only in writing but also in other aspects of your life.[6]

Once your head is in the game—select a research topic. Topic selection requires thought and preliminary research. Many students find the process of choosing a topic to be highly stressful, especially when given the freedom to pick any topic that relates to their major. Understandably, students want guidance, even options when selecting a topic; however, most Capstone professors allow the students to choose any topic of interest so long as it, once again, relates to his or her field of study. Herein you will find some guidance for this broad topic selection.

There are several essential factors the researcher may want to consider when picking a subject to research.

1. First, pick something that you find very interesting as, you will be spending much time researching, studying, preparing, writing about, and presenting this topic. If

---

[6] "Selecting a Topic," *Basic Reading and Writing: Lumen,* accessed September 11, 2021, https://courses.lumenlearning.com/basicreadingandwriting/chapter/outcome-topic-selection/.

you are struggling, consider the "fun fact" you keep in mind about your major. For example, if you go to a family get-together for the holidays and Uncle John says, "tell me something interesting about your schooling...," the fact you have on standby for this moment may be an excellent topic for the Capstone project. Most likely, you know a little about it already, you enjoy talking about it, and you find it interesting enough that you have remembered it despite all else.

Additionally, be sure that you understand the scope of the assignment. In this case, you have a lengthy research paper which is accompanied by an oral presentation. This project is going to require quite a lot of scholarly sources to complete. When selecting a topic, consider the era of the topic. Something exceptionally modern, such as the COVID vaccines, may not appear in many academic publications yet. The lack of publications may be due to the peer-review process and the time it takes the publishing company to publish the work.

On the other hand, do not select an outdated topic unless you compare it to the modern connotations. For example, you do not want to focus on just the benefits of using chloroform during childbirth. In the nineteenth century this was a fairly common practice by physicians to ease labor pains; however, in the twenty-first century physicians understand the dangerous side effects on both mother and child. It is no longer an acceptable method for pain control. It has become outdated; thus, you will need to compare it to modern methods of controlling pain during childbirth to provide a well-rounded paper. Topic selection is a careful balancing act. So, take your time and think about the topic.[7]

2. Next, the pupil will spend time conducting preliminary research on the chosen matter. The scholarship (sources) available on the topic will help you determine whether to pursue the topic further. A Google search followed by a search on the library's homepage could quickly identify if there are significant scholarly sources available. If the search yields low results, meaning there are not enough scholarly articles or texts on the topic, pick something else. Otherwise, you will be riding the struggle bus until you alter the topic out of desperation.

3. After selecting a topic and conducting preliminary research comes a Topic Proposal or Statement of Topic assignment. This assignment aims to inform the instructor of the selected topic and provide information on the research methodology. In other words, what kind of scholarship will you, the researcher, seek out to support the central thesis.

A common issue faced by many students is that their topic is too broad. By conducting this preliminary search for the Topic Proposal, the researcher can begin narrowing and refining the research question, continuing until a narrow thesis is reached. Students often want to write about "the big picture;" however, unless you are writing a novel, you can only write about a small area of that larger picture. For a better understanding, envision your family's living room. The large picture includes a couch, the loveseat, carpet on the floor, a picture window with curtains, and out

---

[7] Ibid., "Selecting a Topic."

that window is a beautiful yard complete with trees and flowers. Now I could write an entire novel if I attempted to detail each aspect of the photo, explaining the significance of each item, its history, and plans for the item. So, instead of attempting to write about everything, I will only write about the couch, providing great detail regarding every little aspect of that couch.

Academically, an example of this comes from an American History course that I instruct students often pick the Civil War as their topic. It is impossible to discuss the entirety of the Civil War adequately and appropriately in a 20-page paper—that topic is too broad. The student could narrow the topic by examining the Battle of Gettysburg instead of the entire war. So, when selecting a topic, think of a small portion of the larger picture.

At this point, you will still be able to narrow and refine the topic through more research. Narrowing and refining the topic can be accomplished through the S.O.C.R.A.P.R. model. To follow the S.O.C.R.A.P.R. model, consider the following.

- **Similarities**: What other events are similar? What can you compare the topic to?

- **Opposites**: What information is available to oppose the topic? Think of a pro and con list.

- **Contrasts**: Evaluate the different opinions on the topic.

- **Relationships**: Consider the different relationships of the topic. What people, places, or organizations have a relationship with it? These relationships are an opportunity for additional information.

- **Anthropomorphisms**: "Attribution of human characteristics to nonhuman entities, objects, or concepts." Thomas the Train is an example.

- **Personifications:** "Giving objects or descriptions human qualities…" An example is the wind screamed….

- **Repetition**: Has the topic [study, event] happened more than once?[8]

A proposal is meant to grasp the audience's attention and illustrate the need for further research. Keep in mind that the paper should offer a new perspective on the matter, not a regurgitation of other scholarship. The student is to create a research question then use primary and secondary forms of scholarship to answer that question.

The typical Topic Selection assignment has several sections that include:

- **Statement of Topic**: This is a brief statement informing the audience of the intended research subject. Keep the topic narrow. The Statement of Topic is not binding. If you decide after some research that you want to approach the argument from a different angle, that is acceptable. You will be required to alter or add to the topic stated as the research project progresses.

- **Preliminary Thesis**: A thesis statement is a sentence that sums up the main point of the paper by answering the proposed research question. It is called a preliminary thesis because, at this point, it is subject to change. The research discovered may lead you in a different direction than initially expected; thus, the thesis statement will need to be altered before the paper can be completed.

---

[8] Ibid., "Selecting a Topic." The Lumen teaching resource provides the concepts of the S.O.C.R.P.R. model that can be used to help narrow a research topic.; "Other APA Guidelines: Anthropomorphism," *Walden University*, September 11, 2021, https://academicguides.waldenu.edu/writingcenter/apa/other/anthropomorphism. Walden University provides additional insight into anthropomorphisms. This term is closely related to personification, which had the potential to be interchangeable in terms of the S.O.C.R.P.R. model.

- **Research Question:** This is a question, not a statement. Do not merely explain the topic you are researching. Pose a question that includes terms like "due to," "resulted from," "required," or terms that show analysis, causation, and close examination. These question or questions are what the researcher intends to answer through scholarship. You are not limited to one sentence for this section.

- **Significance of Topic:** This section can be relatively short, one to two paragraphs, or up to two pages. The length will be prescribed by the instructor, so be sure to check the assignment instructions. The topic's significance examines why the subject is worth researching, how it relates to the chosen discipline, and what the researcher hopes to learn.

- **Bibliography:** Not every Topic Proposal will include a section dedicated to a reference list. It is a good idea to include all sources of scholarship that you have uncovered during the preliminary search. This inclusion is an excellent method for gathering sources for the final paper as many sources will be required. These preliminary sources help shape your argument and understanding of the topic; thus, the authors, along with sources, need to be credited.

Even if the written portion of the topic proposal seems straightforward, picking a topic can be challenging. It would be best to dedicate time and an intelligent look into the topic before making a declaration. Bear in mind, you will be spending quality time on this topic throughout the Capstone class. So, it is critical you enjoy researching, reading, writing, and speaking about the topic. Below is a written example of how a topic proposal should look.

2.11 (Image) The Following is an example of a Topic Proposal in Chicago:

1

Jenn Gmuca
HIUS 530: American Christian Heritage
May 17, 2020
Topic Proposal

A Second Blessing for a Fresh Start: Phoebe Palmer's Evangelical Influence

Throughout the history of Christianity in America, there have been many influential

people. People who have inspired the conversion of hundreds upon thousands of individuals to

the Christian gospel. Despite these numerous members of the Christian faith that potentially

desire the attention of a historian, Phoebe Palmer stands out because of her background, the life

events that led her to pursue a life of holiness in the evangelical circles during revivalism.

Phoebe Palmer is one of the most influential women of the nineteenth-century evangelical

movement due to her inspirational story of conversion, her piety, zeal for writing, and

commitment to social reform.

Palmer was born in New York to a devout Methodist family. Interestingly in her youth,

she asserts that she does not remember when her conversion occurred; this is an experience that

brings the Christian closer to God. According to author Anne Loveland in her article

"Domesticity and Religion in the Antebellum Period," this moment is significant for members of

the Methodist faith. Palmer will experience this moment later in life after being married and

experiencing the tragic loss of her two newborn children. Her conversion or "second blessing,"

as coined by John Wesley occurred in 1837 this occurrence led Palmer to pursue a life of

holiness. Throughout her life, she worked as a missionary, taught in Sunday Schools, worked

with orphans and different levels of volunteerism at orphanages, volunteered at a prison ministry,

and much more. Moreover, Palmer is an accomplished author having published several books.

The most renowned include *The Guide to Holiness* and *The Way of Holiness*, which sold over 24,000 copies.[1]

Palmer dedicated her life's work to the holiness movement of the evangelical cause. Her goal was to spread the word of the gospel; however, it came with a challenge. That challenge was to do spread the word in a patriarchal society, which expected women to dominate the realm of domesticity. Palmer took advance of the wake proceeding revivalism to advance female-driven religious programs. By seizing this opportunity, Palmer can provide women the opportunity for a more prominent social role, which was successful due to the well-defined religious doctrine that was available in texts such as *The Doctrines of the Church; or, Methodism Displayed and Enthusiasm Detected.* Palmer was educated on the doctrines of the Church and understood them well. The combination of knowledge and charming personality made Palmer effective in encouraging women to speak publicly on matters of faith. In the *New York Herald,* Palmer is described as "a warm friend and zealous Christian." Additionally, Palmer was committed to social reform. She worked with organizations such as the salvation army and the temperance movement. Her commitment to such social causes inspired other women to join social reforms, such as Frances Willard, who led the Women's Christian Temperance Union. [2]

---

[1] Anne Loveland, "Domesticity and Religion in the Antebellum Period: The Career of Phoebe Palmer" *The Historian* 39, no. 3 (1977): 456-457.

[2] Theodore Hovet, "Phoebe Palmer's "Altar Phraseology" and the Spiritual Dimension of Woman's Sphere," *The Journal of Religion* 63, no. 3 (1983): 264-265.; Member. *The Doctrines of the Church; or, Methodism Displayed and Enthusiasm Detected.* (New York: Francis Childs and John Swaine, 1793):1-10.; "Funeral of Mrs. Phoebe Palmer," *The New York Herald*, November 06, 1874, Courts Section, 8.; Lucy Lind Hogan, "Negotiating Personhood, Womanhood, and Spiritual Equality: Phoebe Palmer's Defense of the Preaching of Women" *ATQ* 14, no. 3 (2000): 211-212.; "Temperance Women: Miss Willard Presides at the Opening of the W. C. T. U. Convention Honor to Gen. Neal Dow His Birthday Selected as a Time for Holding Prohibition Rallies Maryland is One of the States in which the Union made the Largest Membership Gain Last Year –Lady Somerset Sends a Greeting From Across the Sea." *The Sun* (1837-1994), Nov 14, 1896. 8.

18

In summation, the historical significance of Phoebe Palmer begins with her Methodist up brining and her "second blessing" then continues with her life's dedication to the evangelical movements and social reforms of the nineteenth century. She is one of the most influential women of this period and has left a lasting impression of America's Christian Heritage.

4

Bibliography

"Funeral of Mrs. Phoebe Palmer." *The New York Herald,* November 06, 1874, Courts Section, 8.

Haight, A. "Status and Feminine Leadership in a Mid-Nineteenth-Century Evangelical Community: Phoebe Palmer and the Holiness Connexion, 1835-1874." Order No. U354541, University of Oxford United Kingdom, 1985.

Hogan, Lucy Lind. "Negotiating Personhood, Womanhood, and Spiritual Equality: Phoebe Palmer's Defense of the Preaching of Women." *ATQ* 14, no. 3 (2000): 211-226.

Hovet, Theodore. "Phoebe Palmer's "Altar Phraseology" and the Spiritual Dimension of Woman's Sphere." *The Journal of Religion* 63, no. 3 (1983): 264-80.

Loveland, Anne C. "Domesticity and Religion in the Antebellum Period: The Career of Phoebe Palmer." *The Historian* 39, no. 3 (1977): 455-71.

Member. *The Doctrines of the Church; or, Methodism Displayed and Enthusiasm Detected.* New York: Francis Childs and John Swaine, 1793.

McDonald, William. "Naked Faith: The Mystical Theology of Phoebe Palmer." *Journal of Ecumenical Studies* 45, no. 1 (Winter 2010): 164.

Stevens, Abel. *The History of the Religious Movement of the Eighteenth Century Called Methodism, Considered in its Different Denominational Forms, and its Relations to British and American Protestantism.* Vol. 2. New York: Carlton & Porter, 1858-1861. *Sabin Americana: History of the Americas, 1500-1926* (accessed May 16, 2020). https://link-gale-com.ezproxy.liberty.edu/apps/doc/CY0104206675/SABN?u=vic_liberty&sid=SABN&xid=e7787144.

"Temperance Women: Miss Willard Presides at the Opening of the W. C. T. U. Convention Honor to Gen. Neal Dow His Birthday Selected as a Time for Holding Prohibition Rallies Maryland is One of the States in which the Union made the Largest Membership Gain Last Year –Lady Somerset Sends a Greeting From Across the Sea." *The Sun (1837-1994),* Nov 14, 1896. 8.

2.2 Research Proposal

Writing a solid academic research paper is like assembling a structure out of building blocks. Everything rests on the foundation. In academic writing, everything rests on the thesis statement and research question. The thesis statement answers the research question. Once the researcher has a solid foundation [thesis statement], begin adding more and more informational blocks to create a solid structured argument. The informational blocks will be gathered throughout the following steps: it is essential to remember that the researcher is not rebuilding the foundational thesis if the research takes a turn; instead, additional information may be needed to help support the central argument. Like the rows of a block tower, each assignment builds upon the previous towards completing the final product.

The purpose of a Research Proposal is to grab the attention of your intended audience to demonstrate why the topic is worth researching and is vital to the field. Again, you are not regurgitating information that you read: instead, you are contributing to the field by reading the work of other scholars and experts then arriving at your conclusion. Consider the breadth and depth of the topic. In other words, ask how you will make your paper stand out from the rest and how will it contribute [add] to the field of study.

The Research Proposal expands the Topic Selection, including several existing sections and several new categories. The student is to revise, alter, and expand upon the existing sections from one assignment to the next.

Here are the sections of a Research Proposal.

- **Title**: Create a working title, and it should grab the attention of the reader. Consider the reasons you have selected a book to read for pleasure. Did it have a catchy title? Was that the reason you initially picked it up? Start working on an attention grabber.

- **Preliminary Thesis Statement:** The preliminary thesis statement was established in the previous assignment. [See Topic Proposal for more details.] Remember that the thesis statement answers the research question. This statement is an overview of what the paper will include. At this point, edit and revise if necessary. It may also be necessary for the researcher to narrow the topic further.

- **Significance of Topic/Introduction:** What makes this topic worth additional research? This section will add context so that the reader understands the informational direction the author is heading. Bear in mind that this section can be short or long, depending on the instructor. Generally, the Significance of Topic is two pages in length. It is essential to carefully develop this section due to the possibility of including it in the introduction of the final paper. You will need to provide in-text citations giving credit to referenced sources throughout this section. Like the introduction of your paper, this should be easy-to-understand information about the topic which helps introduce a general audience to the central thesis.[9]

- **Research Plan:** It is time to design a plan to accomplish all the research promptly. You will be required to include a specified number of sources in your final paper. For example, you may be required to have ten primary sources and ten secondary sources.

---

[9] "How to Write a Thesis Proposal," *Columbia,* accessed September 11, 2021, https://www.ldeo.columbia.edu/~martins/sen_res/how_to_thesis_proposal.html

How will you gather these sources? Will it be a trip to the archives, the library, or online? Are you conducting an interview which will need transcription? How much time should you allow for transcription?

Next, consider the availability of sources. Are all the required sources available free online or at the school's library? Will you need to acquire any sources through the interlibrary loan (ILL) process? Do you know how to request an ILL? The request can be made via the library's website or by visiting the library requesting the help of the excellent librarians. Librarians love to help with research. It is essential to befriend the library staff. They are a precious resource for finding information.

By developing a time management plan and adhering to it, the researcher should have enough time to ensure proper formatting, proper accreditation, and accurate grammatical skills. A major mistake is many students think that there is enough time in the semester to do things "later." The semester goes faster than anticipated, and life gets in the way. Be diligent.

- **Preliminary Sources:** For this assignment, you will be required to find a specified number of primary sources or initial research. Instructors require five to ten primary sources, depending on the length of your paper. The instructions provided by the instructor will outline the exact number of primary and secondary sources you are required to include. Students must fulfill all the assignment requirements to earn a passing grade.

Remember, you are writing an academic paper, so you want scholarship [resources] that are peer-reviewed and reliable. There is that word, reliable! Pay close attention to who is writing the source. Examine why the author is considered an expert on the subject. For example, if John Smith graduated from Harvard University with a Ph.D.

in Revolutionary History, his article on the Declaration of Independence is most likely reliable. On the other hand, if Bill Smith creates a website blog after watching *National Treasure*, he is probably not a reliable scholarly source. Knowing the reliability of the author indicates the reliability of the source.

Refresher on Primary and Secondary Sources: *(Primary and secondary sources will be discussed in further detail in Chapter 3, Section 1)*

A potentially silly way to remember the difference between a primary and secondary source is the saying, "I heard it straight from the horse's mouth." A primary source comes from someone who directly witnessed the event [the talking horse]. If a direct witness or the talking horse itself writes about the event, then it is primary. On the contrary, if your grandpa told you about his cousin's talking horse, you are getting too far removed from the actual event; thus, it is secondary.

I am attempting to illustrate with this slightly silly analogy that a primary source is a first-hand account. In contrast, a secondary source accounts for a person who has read the primary [first-hand] account.

It seems relatively straightforward. Identifying an actual source as primary or secondary can be confusing, and anything that does not fit into the first-hand account category is a secondary source. Therefore, when in doubt, ask a librarian or instructor for help.

- **Literature Review:** This section discusses source reliability and the research methodology. *(Please see section 3.3 for further details on Research Methodology.)* After reading, examining, and verifying reliability *(see section 3.2 for more detail on verifying reliability)*, you can ascertain the source's usefulness as it pertains to the paper's central thesis and discuss your primary research methodology in this section.

This section is roughly two paragraphs in length. The researchers should name at least one primary and one secondary source, discuss the source's content, and elaborate on the author. The listed sources should be crucial to the central thesis and will be referenced frequently throughout. To learn the validity of the expert, one should complete an internet search, and author reliability is essential thus should not be overlooked.

Do not let the extent of the Research Proposal intimidate you. This assignment will prove helpful throughout your career. A business major will write business proposals, a museum curator may write exhibit proposals, and a physician may write grant proposals for research. The key takeaway from a proposal is its purpose—to grab the intended audience's attention and convince them of the importance of the work.

2.21 (image) The Following is an example of a Research Proposal in Chicago:

Jenn Gmuca
August 29, 2020
HUIS 820: Research in the Civil War
Topic Proposal

Alleghany Arsenal Explosion:
Pittsburgh's Contribution to the Bloodiest Day of the Civil War

The American Civil War is renowned for violent battles, heroic soldiers, and untimely deaths. Often neglected from memory are the heroes off the battlefields, those individuals, which made the war possible. Men, women, and children who worked tirelessly to contribute to the war effort behind the scenes and sadly killed while attempting to keep the soldiers on the front-lines supplied with the ammunition they so desperately needed to continue fighting; the women and children who worked at the Allegheny Arsenal a shining example of community members who worked to keep the war effort afloat. The Allegheny Arsenal tragically exploded on September 17, 1862, contributing to the Civil War's bloodiest day, negatively affecting the Union's war effort, and forever changing the region.

The Allegheny Arsenal is significant to the Civil War as it produced large amounts of ammunition for Union troops. Since Pittsburgh has the natural resources required to produce the ammunition, the region became one of the largest suppliers during the war. Additionally, the arsenal was located a few miles from Pittsburgh's River system, making shipping accessible.[1] The importance of the Allegheny Arsenal to the Northern Civil War effort will allow research into military, social, and political history.

Fortunately, there appear to be many primary sources nearby for this research project since the arsenal explosion is local. After initial research, there appear to be few books written on the topic the main books found are by author James Wudarczyk *Pittsburgh's Forgotten*

---

[1] Tom Powers and James Wudarczyk, *Behind the Scenes of the Allegheny Arsenal Explosion*, (The Historical Society of Pennsylvania: University of Pennsylvania Press, 2013),43.

Allegheny Arsenal and Tom Powers and James Wudarczyk, *Behind the Scenes of the Allegheny Arsenal Explosion.* The National Archives Website has a collection of primary sources on the arsenal; further, the Arsenal Park is in Lawrenceville Pittsburgh, Pennsylvania, which is within traveling distance.[2]   The preliminary search for this project yields promising results in terms of volume and variety of primary and secondary sources.

---

[2] Powers and Wudarczyk, 2013. In this text, authors Powers and Wudarczyk attempt to explain the possible causes of the Allegheny Arsenal explosion and provide background information about the institution itself.; James Wudarczyk, *Pittsburgh's Forgotten Allegheny Arsenal,* (Closson Press, 1999.), this text is unavailable online; thus, it would need to be obtained through interlibrary loan. It is the first book to cover the history of the arsenal. "Allegheny Arsenal," National Archives, last modified August 15, 2016. https://www.archives.gov/philadelphia/exhibits/allegheny-arsenal/allegheny-arsenal.html; The National Archives provides digitally archived documents blueprints of the arsenal and newspaper clipping of the explosion that will be beneficial to this research project. Thomas Harper, "Arsenal Park Pittsburgh, Pennsylvania," Accessed August 30, 2020, https://www.atlasobscura.com/places/arsenal-park; This website provides information about the Arsenal memorial site regarding location and history.

3

Bibliography

"Allegheny Arsenal." *National Archives.* Last Modified August 15, 2016.
 https://www.archives.gov/philadelphia/exhibits/allegheny-arsenal/allegheny-arsenal.html

Harper, Thomas. "Arsenal Park Pittsburgh, Pennsylvania." Accessed August 30, 2020.
 https://www.atlasobscura.com/places/arsenal-park

Powers, Tom, and James Wudarczyk. *Behind the Scenes of the Allegheny Arsenal Explosion.*
 The Historical Society of Pennsylvania: University of Pennsylvania Press, 2013.

Wudarczyk, James. *Pittsburgh's Forgotten Allegheny Arsenal.* Closson Press, 1999.

2.3 Research Prospectus

The Research Prospectus, admittedly, is quite like the Research Proposal. Each instructor will assign these differently; at times, they will be interchangeable. Typically, the Research Prospectus is assigned at the master's degree level while the Research Proposal occurs in undergraduate studies. There has recently been an influx of Research Prospectus Assignments associated with Capstone courses; thus, the inclusion of this assignment is done with the intent of helping students who are new to prospectus writing navigate this unchartered territory.

Within the prospectus, the researcher is charged with presenting a research question or questions that will be examined. There will be potential complications throughout this process. The prospectus is an excellent tool to help prepare for the problems that might arise. Completing a prospectus is not a task that can be accomplished in one sitting or overnight; it will require work.[10]

Moving forward, the elements of the prospectus are somewhat like the research proposal, but as you can imagine, the prospectus is more detailed. The Research Prospectus must illustrate the thesis statement, overview the research question, provide boundaries on the inquiry, describe the research methodology employed, and discuss the potential problems or difficulties encountered while researching.[11]

---

[10] William Cronon, "Writing a Research Prospectus," accessed September 11, 2021, https://www.williamcronon.net/handouts/Writing_A_Research_Prospectus.pdf

[11] *Prospectus Manual*, (Lynchburg, VA: Liberty University, 2008), 3.

Research methodology involves gathering sources, examining the types of sources searched for, and writing a brief description of those sources. For example, you may be looking for diary or journal entries of an individual or datasets from a business's financial statements.

A Research Prospectus typically has six sections.

- **Selected Topic:** The topic should be getting refined at this point. (See Topic Proposal for more detail on Thesis Statement)

- **Research Question/Thesis Statement:** A thesis statement is a sentence that sums up the paper's main point. The thesis answers the research question or a designated prompt through research. Edit and refine the statement with each assignment.

- **Explanation of Significance:** This extends the Significance of Topic from the Topic Proposal. You, the researcher, will treat the Explanation of Significances much like the introduction to your final paper; it will examine the parameters for the topic, explain why the topic is worth researching, and add depth to your field. The length of this section is roughly two pages; however, be sure to verify with the instructor. It is common for instructors to alter the length of sections of the Research Prospectus.

- **Research Prospectus:** In this section, the writer will examine the research methodology used. In other words, what kinds of sources are you searching for—primary sources such as diaries, newspaper clippings, journals, medical studies, datasets? Secondary sources like peer-reviewed journal articles, books? Name the sources that you will rely most heavily upon and describe the author's credibility. This section is essential because it forces the researcher to examine the quality of scholarship located. The quality of scholarship is paramount when students are hyper-focused on the number of sources, not quality.

Additionally, this section allows the researcher to note any issues that may be anticipated or encounter. For instance, is there a newspaper clipping necessary to your thesis that you do not have access to? How is the writer going to overcome it? Is there travel involved for research that is not practical? How will be researcher go about contacting that organization? Students seem to have an aversion to traveling for research, even if that travel is just to the campus library. However, it is not always feasible to conduct all your research online. There may be significantly more substantial resources in the archives or the library. So, get out of your comfort zone and go to the library. Archivists and librarians are experts on their collections. They will be able to locate a wide variety of sources. Plus, they enjoy their work! Let them help!

- **Research Plan:** The Research Plan is a plan of attack for tackling a paper of this magnitude. My students use their imaginations for this portion of the assignment due to the aversion to physically going to research. This section is roughly two paragraphs. Discuss how you will obtain all the research you need. Will you require interlibrary loans, how long do they take to arrive, and is there a fee associated with the loan? How will you pay for the material or travel that is required? Write a grant? This section is designed to get the students thinking and planning to gather their sources and write their assignments becomes manageable.

Further, you should incorporate a few sentences in your writing process. The writing process is equally crucial for time management. Consider your schedule, plan to complete the assignment, and stick to it. Otherwise, procrastination will win, and you will be pulling an all-nighter to submit a subpar paper.

- **Preliminary Bibliography:** The Preliminary Bibliography, References, or Work Cited (depending on your writing style) is a shortlist of the sources you have gathered thus far. Usually, your instructor will provide you with a set number of primary and secondary sources required. Make sure you have cited the sources in the proper format. Take the time to do it correctly now, and it will save you the time of re-creating the citations later.

At the risk of stating an unpopular opinion, do not waste your time with citation generators. The citation styles change often, and the software is often not up to date, or it is wrong. It is in your best interest to reference the citation style manual and create the citation from scratch. Once you become good at this, it is faster than correcting a generated citation.

2.31 (image) The Following is an example of a Research Prospectus in Chicago:

Research Prospectus:

A Second Blessing for a Fresh Start:

Phoebe Palmer's Evangelical Influence

Jennifer Gmuca

HIUS 530: American Christian Heritage

May 29, 2020

Selected Topic

The proposed topic is Phoebe Palmer's evangelical influence on Methodism in nineteenth-century American.

Research Question

What early events led caused Phoebe Palmers to become a significant influence on the Methodist denomination, and what powerful effects did she have on other followers?

Preliminary Thesis Statement

Phoebe Palmer is one of the most influential women of the nineteenth-century evangelical movement due to her inspirational story of conversion, piety, zeal for writing, and commitment to social reform.

Research Prospectus

The research paper will focus on Phoebe Palmer's devotion to Christianity and her evangelical influences throughout nineteenth-century America. Palmer's story begins with her conversion, which led to a life of holiness, coupled with a commitment to both the Methodist denominations and its community. This portion of the paper will include Palmer's background with further explanation of John Wesley's doctrine. Additionally, Palmer's contributions, both written and social, will be explored, as well as how these contributions influenced others to become involved in the Great Awakenings, such as Francis Willard.

The research will require many sources, both primary and secondary. The primary sources will include books written by Palmer, such as *The Way of Holiness*, and publications by different authors such as *The Doctrines of the Church*. Secondary sources appear to be plentiful on Palmer. A few secondary sources include Patricia Bizzell, "Frances Willard, Phoebe Palmer, and the Ethos of the Methodist Woman Preacher," and Elaine Heath *Naked Faith*. This list is a sample of the bibliography listed below, which is not extensive. More research will need to be conducted to complete this research paper with adequate sourcing.

Explanation of Historical Significance

Phoebe Palmer is one of the founders of the Holiness Movement of the Methodist Community during the Second Great Awaking in nineteenth-century America. Her evangelical influences encouraged social reforms that helped shape society for years to come. Further, Palmer was an activist for women gaining a more prominent role in religion. She took advantage of revivalism to make advances for women in this arena. As an accomplished writer, Palmer was able to spread the word of the gospel eloquently, helping others experience their moments of conversion, which was vital to the Methodist denomination.

Research Plan

No travel is required to complete this research project. All the research required can be accomplished via Liberty University's Jerry Farewell Library website or other source repositories. This project will require time management and interlibrary loan services to accomplish since interlibrary loan services typically do not incur a charge and can be accomplished electronically within a few days that task should be accomplished within a week. The next steps to complete this project will be to collect and evaluate the primary and secondary sources, several of which need to be obtained via interlibrary loan. Then the research paper will enter the rough draft portion of the writing process, followed by the editing process, before finalization, and submitted via Blackboard on its assigned due date.

3

Bibliography

Bizzell, Patricia. "Frances Willard, Phoebe Palmer, and the Ethos of the Methodist Woman Preacher." *Rhetoric Society Quarterly* 36, no. 4 (2006): 377-398.

"Funeral of Mrs. Phoebe Palmer." *The New York Herald,* November 06, 1874, Courts Section, 8.

Haight, A. "Status and Feminine Leadership in a Mid-Nineteenth-Century Evangelical Community: Phoebe Palmer and the Holiness Connexion, 1835-1874." Order No. U354541, University of Oxford United Kingdom, 1985.

Heath, Elaine A. *Naked Faith.* Cambridge: James Clarke & Co, 2009.

Hogan, Lucy Lind. "Negotiating Personhood, Womanhood, and Spiritual Equality: Phoebe Palmer's Defense of the Preaching of Women." *ATQ* 14, no. 3 (2000): 211-226.

Hovet, Theodore. "Phoebe Palmer's "Altar Phraseology" and the Spiritual Dimension of Woman's Sphere." *The Journal of Religion* 63, no. 3 (1983): 264-80.

Jones, Charles Edwin. "The Posthumous Pilgrimage of Phoebe Palmer." *Methodist History* 35, no. 4 (1997): 203-213.

Loveland, Anne C. "Domesticity and Religion in the Antebellum Period: The Career of Phoebe Palmer." *The Historian* 39, no. 3 (1977): 455-71.

Member. *The Doctrines of the Church; or, Methodism Displayed and Enthusiasm Detected.* New York: Francis Childs and John Swaine, 1793.

McDonald, William. "Naked Faith: The Mystical Theology of Phoebe Palmer." *Journal of Ecumenical Studies* 45, no. 1 (Winter 2010): 164.

Palmer, Phoebe. *The Way of Holiness with Notes by the Way; being a Narrative of Religious Experience Resulting from a Determination to be a Bible Christian.* New York: Printed for the Author, 1854.

Stevens, Abel. *The History of the Religious Movement of the Eighteenth Century Called Methodism, Considered in its Different Denominational Forms, and its Relations to British and American Protestantism.* Vol. 2. New York: Carlton & Porter, 1858-1861. *Sabin Americana: History of the Americas, 1500-1926* (accessed May 16, 2020). https://link-gale-com.ezproxy.liberty.edu/apps/doc/CY0104206675/SABN?u=vic_liberty&sid=SABN&xid=e7787144.

"Temperance Women: Miss Willard Presides at the Opening of the W. C. T. U. Convention Honor to Gen. Neal Dow His Birthday Selected as a Time for Holding Prohibition Rallies Maryland is One of the States in which the Union made the Largest Membership Gain

CHAPTER 3: TIME TO WRITE!

The time has come for you to embark on the enormous journey of research, development, and articulation of a research paper. It is an inspiring point in every student's academic career to place that cap-stone at the top of your list of accomplishments. By the time you have completed the Capstone journey; you will have collected memories that will stick with you. *Wait, How Many Pages? The Bedrock for Conquering Capstone* is designed to prevent these lovely memories from becoming terrible nightmares.

Lastly, this section examines the elements that make annotated bibliographies exceptional, useful outlines, and final papers exceptional. As stated earlier, you are completing a Capstone project. Throughout this project, you will have to demonstrate various skills that you have learned during your education. Placing the cap-stone on your education is extremely rewarding. As with all good things, it requires hard work and dedication.

3.1 Annotated Bibliography

Another popular assignment in advanced research is the annotated bibliography. While it can appear insurmountable at first glance, it is relatively simple to complete; however, it can be time consuming. Do not underestimate the amount necessary to complete this task correctly. Personally, this is my favorite assignment. Before you scoff at this facetious statement, allow me to explain. The annotated bibliography forces you to read each source early in the research process, which most people put off to the final hour. When researching, you probably do a quick search, read only enough to know if the source pertains to your topic, then save it for later. The annotated bibliography forces you to read the collected material, providing you with the opportunity to critically analyze the usefulness of the scholarship— simultaneously providing the opportunity for further research if necessary. The bonus feature of the assignment is having critical analysis and the literature review completed before struggling to assemble the final product. According to Cornell University's LibGuide on "How to Prepare an Annotated Bibliography," the purpose of this assignment is to "… inform the reader of the relevance, accuracy, and quality of the sources cited." The evaluation of sources is accomplished by using "…the application of various intellectual skills: concise exposition, succinct analysis, and informed library research."[12]

Understanding the essence of the assignment is critical to ascertaining the various structural differences in the annotations themselves. This assignment consists of a cover page followed by a properly formatted bibliographical list of scholarly literature. Depending on the citation style of your discipline, this bibliographical list may be referred to as a bibliography, references, or work cited. Pay close attention to the contrasting requirements regarding the type of sources [secondary

---

[12] "How to Prepare an Annotated Bibliography: The Annotated Bibliography," *Cornell University Library*, May 5, 2021, https://guides.library.cornell.edu/annotatedbibliography

or primary] required. Failure to adequately display appropriate sources will negatively impact your grade. Moreover, the type of sources that are required may vary between articles and books.

Typically, students must list primary and secondary sources under subheadings with a further subdivision for articles and books. All assignment requirements can be located on the instructions and rubric. The list of sources must be in alphabetical order, even if there are subheadings. Failure to alphabetize is an easy mistake, so be cautious always to ensure that the list is in alphabetical order.

The proper formatting of this assignment is often confusing and one of the main questions by students. As with everything else, each citation style recommends a different format. Do some research on what your citation style recommends. A commonality of all citation styles is the hanging indent. A hanging indent is when the first line is not indented [remaining flush with the left side of the page], and all subsequent lines are indented. A handing indent can be accomplished in one of two ways. First, highlight the entry that requires the special indentation, right-click on the mouse moving to paragraphs, then on to indentation section, to special entry, there you will find a drop-down box for hanging indent. The second method is to highlight the item then using the bottom of the alignment tab to toggle over half an inch, creating the hanging indent.

In addition to the list of scholarship, each source will be accompanied by an annotation. The annotation is an explanation or note about the source's content. You are critically evaluating the source's content as it pertains to the central thesis of your paper. Moreover, you want to examine the author's credibility. Plus, the annotation length depends on the instructor's preference; however, two to three sentences is the minimum.

The literature review comes down to two critical processes: the initial appraisal and content analysis. To adequately complete this analysis, use the C.R.A.A.P. method. The C.R.A.A.P. method is an excellent way to ascertain the validity and relevance of scholarship. C.R.A.A.P. stands for currency, relevance, authority, accuracy, and purpose.[13]

- **Initial Appraisal**: The initial appraisal is the first look at the source. The appraisal will help determine if the article, book, or website relates to the paper's central thesis. If the source seems worthwhile, then the researcher can critically analyze the content.

- **Content Analysis:** Once the student has done the initial appraisal of the source, concluding that the evidence will be helpful within the final product, the next step is to analyze the content of the scholarship. This analysis examines research methodology, use of scholarship, and ideology. Be sure to take notes as you are reading. Notation is helpful during the writing stage of the annotation.

To properly utilize the initial appraisal and content analysis process of evaluating sources, apply the C.R.A.A.P. test.

- **Currency:** "When was the information published?"[14] Examining the publication date will help you determine if the source is up-to-date and into what category it will fall — primary or secondary sources. Currency is essential to understanding to most up-to-

---

[13] "Source Analysis," *Basic Reading and Writing: Lumen Learning*, accessed September 9, 2021, https://courses.lumenlearning.com/suny-basicreadingwriting/chapter/research-tips/

[14] Ibid., "Source Analysis."

date theory of the topic. The researcher wants to avoid utilizing outdated information as the new assertions may discredit the scope of the antiquated source.

For example, if you are a business major researching the development of a corporation, you need to have various sources dating on a timeline. However, suppose you are a biology major examining the effects of Zoloft [an anti-depression and anti-anxiety medication] on the brain. In that case, you will want to find sources that date around the initial medical study. Information before the case study is likely irrelevant to the scope of your topic. The range for publication date is based on the individual subject matter. The differing date ranges are a unique aspect of research methodology. The periods are personalized to the individual topics, so each classroom member is potentially searching in a different era, which will lend to variety. Unfortunately, there is no blanket statement regarding date ranges for primary and secondary sources, making research more challenging.

- **Relevance:** "How relevant to your goals is the information?"[15] Does the text add new information? Does it update any other source that you have identified? How does it contribute to existing research? As a researcher, you will need various facts or concepts to reach the breadth and depth that a Capstone paper requires. Recall the block building analogy; you take these informational blocks [texts] and build upon each other to reach a final product.

Do not forget to evaluate the writing style of the author. Is it easy to read, does it flow, or is it choppy—confusing? The goal here is to learn about writing styles, utilizing this knowledge to develop your own. By evaluating the sources, you can determine your unique preferences.

---

[15] Ibid., "Source Analysis."

Is the author repetitive? Repetition is not necessarily a negative aspect of writing, and perhaps the author is attempting to drive home a point. This text, for example, is repetitive, but the goal is to teach you how to complete these assignments so that you gain the necessary bedrock for conquering Capstone—again, repetition.

Lastly, take a deeper dive into the publisher of the text. If it is an article, investigate the journal in which it is published. Is the journal a scholarly journal? Keep in mind that a journal is another name for a magazine. So, if you are looking up the journal information, you are looking for the "magazine" that would have printed the article had it been in print. Think of *Time* magazine; the articles are published within magazine's pages.

- **Authority:** "How well does the author of the information know the information?"[16] Investigate the author. Search for the author to find out why he or she should be considered an expert on the subject. What is the author's educational and professional background? Why is the author considered an expert on this subject? Make a note of this information because you can add it to your paper. It illustrates author credibility, adds transitional introductions of scholarship, and [let us be honest] adds length to the paper. When writing a long paper, every word helps, and it also creates depth.

  Next, look at the publisher. The publication company provides a significant clue as to the reliability of the source. If the publisher is a University Press, then the source is most likely scholarly, and peer viewed. Keep in mind that just because the publisher is reliable does not guarantee the source is as well. That is why additional research is necessary. Additional research is beneficial when the source is found through a general search engine, such as Google, instead of the school's databases.

---

[16] Ibid., "Source Analysis."

- **Accuracy:** "How reliable is the information?"[17] Use objective reasoning to examine the information that is presented. What is that information based on: facts, opinion, and/or propaganda? Information based on facts can be proven through statistics, datasets, or other forms of evidence. When an author produces a fact-based article, the author examines the facts, coming to his or her conclusion based on the findings. Therefore, researchers use primary source documents to assess the fact without bias—reaching their conclusion. This process is the reason that you have primary and secondary sources in a paper. The researcher will examine the verifiable information of the primary source then evaluate secondary interpretations.

  Moreover, the researcher must determine if the text is aligned to support or oppose the thesis. It is vital to included counter-evidence to present a well-rounded interpretation of information. Otherwise, you will construct a one-sided argument on the subject matter.

- **Purpose:** "Why does this information exist in this way?"[18] For whom is the publication intended? A scholarly audience or a general audience? You, as an upperclassman, are an informed audience. You have two to three years of education on the subject matter that you will be writing on. Remember that it is possible to get a Capstone professor with a different educational background than you, so you will need to explain anything that is not common knowledge within your text. Thoroughly explaining the content of the paper will also prepare you for the presentation of your material.

  The substance of the annotation is directly affected by the timing of its assignment, which means that your instructor may assign the annotated bibliography at the

---

[17] Ibid., "Source Analysis."

[18] Ibid., "Source Analysis."

beginning, middle, or end of the writing process. Before examining this, you must understand what an annotation is and how that differs from an abstract. Cornell University defines an abstract as "purely descriptive summaries often found at the beginning of scholarly journal articles or in periodical indexes." The annotation, on the other hand, is a more complex analysis. It is "descriptive and critical... describe[ing] the author's point of view, authority, or clarity and appropriateness of expression."[19]

Now that you have a clearer picture of what an annotation consists of through the application of the C.R.A.A.P test, let us examine the difference in content depending on when the assignment is due.

- **Theoretical Annotation:** In some classes, the professor assigns the annotated bibliography directly following the topic proposal. Early distribution is done to force students to collect all their research upfronts. The main question becomes, "how do you write about an unread source?" The answer is in theory. Based on the initial evaluation, you write about what you expect to find in the article or book [see above for initial appraisal]. Using statements like, "In this article, I expect to find...." You base your annotations on the abstracts of the scholarship. Then as research progresses, the bibliography will be altered, removing, or adding sources that support the central thesis of the project. Typically, the earlier the annotated bibliography is assigned, the shorter the annotations.

---

[19] Ibid., "How to Prepare an Annotated Bibliography."

The theoretical annotation allows students to have more time with the sources once they are located. In addition to that, it helps students formulate a thesis statement. Recall that the thesis statement answers the research question, creating the foundation of informational building blocks. Understanding more about the topic will help you gain perspective as to the direction of the paper. Gaining a working knowledge is particularly important on new subject matters. If the writer has little experience on the subject, creating an annotated bibliography will provide them with a better understanding.

2.41 (example) Below is an annotated bibliographic entry in Chicago:

Powers, Tom. "The Arsenal Explosion." *Lawrenceville Historical Society* (March 2012). http://lawrencevillehistoricalsociety.com/face-of-a-tragedy/

This article is a descriptive map illustrating the explosion, which shows where the horse and wagon were to the powder barrels. This scholarship will be beneficial to the project by illustrating the possible explanations for the detonation.

- **Basic Annotation:** If the annotated bibliography is assigned in the middle of the semester, students will read some of their sources after the topic and research proposals. Students will write a basic annotation only examining the substance of the source itself, using some of the information collected in the content analysis. "In this article, x, y, and z are examined." The basic annotation is due to the lack of time to properly examine the entirety of the source as it pertains to the central thesis. Meaning, you have read the source but have not completed the C.R.A.A.P. test. You will need to be mindful of relevance to the thesis and author credibility before using the source within your paper.

2.42 (example) Below is an annotated bibliographic entry in Chicago:

Barton, Clara. "More Help Needed." *The Daily Inter Ocean* (Chicago, IL) June 25, 1889.

Clara Barton, the President of the National Red Cross, wrote a letter requesting more help for the city of Johnstown. This letter provides an update on the wreckage removal after the flood.

- **CRAAP Proof Annotation:** Finally, if the annotated bibliography is assigned just before the rough draft, you have the fantastic opportunity to use it as a precursor for your paper. At this point, you have had significant time with the bibliographic list, so the annotations are expected to be quite detailed. You are expected to include the information from both the initial evaluation and the content analysis—the entire list of C.R.A.A.P. At this point, your annotations will be longer to include the following information:
  - **Citation:** Use the citation style suitable for your discipline. Include a citation of the text that would appear in the bibliography, reference list, or work cited of your paper. Be sure to alphabetize and categorize sources.

Then create a new paragraph just under the citation and include the following:

  - **Methodology:** what is the author's research methodology? Research methodology is a fancy way of asking what kind of sources the author reference within the text. Primary sources such as diaries, legal documents, medical studies, or datasets? Or secondary sources, such as journal articles?

- o **Credibility:** Write about the credibility of the author. Who is the author? Why is he or she an authority? What is the author's educational and professional background?

- o **Summary:** Summarize the text. What is the text about?

- o **Evaluation-** Present your evaluation of the text. Is the information presented well? Is it confusing?

- o **Thesis Support:** Finally, how does this text support the thesis of your paper? How will it benefit the content of it? Is it supporting or opposing information?

2.43 (example) example of an annotated bibliographic entry in Chicago:

Bryan, Maria. *Tokens of Affection: Letters of a Planter's Daughter in the Old South.* Edited by Carol Blesser. Georgia: University of George Press, 1996.

In Tokens of Affection: Letters of a Planter's Daughter in the Old South (1996), editor Carol Blesser presents Marian Bryan's letters to her married sister Julian Lynn Bryan Cumming. Bryan did not want her sister to save her letters or show them to anyone; this candidness may have allowed Bryan to write more openly and honestly about her personal experiences. Under the assumption that her letters were private, assumably, Bryan would not be concerned with proper social conduct when discussing a woman's experiences about marriage and childbirth. During this time, women were not to speak or write ill of the childbirth experience since it was God's will for women to experience the pains and discomforts of labor. Additionally, Bryan discussed details of life as a mistress during the nineteenth century Antebellum Georgia. Her collection of letters helps illustrate the changes in social pressures of marriage, childbirth, and motherhood during this time thus showing the struggles and triumphs of the study of medicine.

Annotated Bibliographies can be a significant undertaking, so be sure to allocate the appropriate amount of time to complete the assignment.

48

3.2 Creating an Outline

It is time to start assembling your final paper. It would help if you had all the required sources gathered; however, be open to looking for additional scholarship if a section of your paper lacks substantial support.

The first step to writing a rough draft is to create an outline of the final paper. Every student has his or her style and method of examining the sources for fit within the content. The purpose of the outline is to organize your thoughts into a structure that flows seamlessly. Students who create outlines are successful in their writing assignments due to the organization of their thoughts.

Outlines can be created in many ways; typically, they are accomplished by making a bullet point list of main points that the author wanted to incorporate into the paper. While the outline is an invaluable tool, it becomes more difficult to outline and organize large amounts of research. Once you have a list of general main points to examine, it is time to organize the mountain of research you have collected.[20]

One method of organizing sources is printing out the sources or making note cards indicating the original location. I make note cards with the author's last name, text title, and a bulleted list of the information I intend to include. Not only does this help with locating the information, but also it helps with paraphrases. Paraphrasing is an issue with many students because students do not get physically far enough away from the source. Yes, I mean physically removed from the source. Our brains pick up more information than we realize just by looking at

---

[20] "Writing a Research Paper: Exploring the Process of Writing a Research Paper," *Arendelle Library: Piedmont University,* accessed September 11, 2021, https://library.piedmont.edu/c.php?g=521348&p=3564598

the text. This detection is done throughout peripheral awareness, a process of the brain that detects and processes information in our peripheral vision without us being fully aware of the reception of information.[21] So, when attempting to paraphrase information that is still within your peripheral vision, you are more likely to regurgitate the exact information without intent. This act could result in the accusation of plagiarism. It is best to read the information, regardless of the format, then physically move it away from you to attempt to paraphrase. The fear of plagiarism is why making note cards for the outlining process with bullet points is an excellent tactic. It removes the source from your vision line, thus reducing the peripheral awareness and the subconscious temptation to repeat the text. I take the note cards that I have created and lay them out in front of me, categorizing them into like topics. Once I have put all the sources into categories, I can create an outline that mimics the flow of information in the notecard piles.

There are many ways to categorize the information in the essay's body; however, it is crucial to present the information to be fluid. The information will be telling a story that supports the thesis statement, the answer to the research question. Moreover, you will want to include counter opinions to show that you have conducted a well-rounded search of the sources available on the topic.

---

[21] Robert Chia, "Peripheral Awareness in Strategic Thinking," *Aes-thesis* 1, no. 2 (2007), 62-65.

3.3 Rough Draft and Peer Review

It is time to put pen to paper; well, it is more like fingertips to keys. The rough draft is a popular assignment for Capstone Seminar. According to the Elftmann Student Success Center at Dunwoody College of Technology, "The sole purpose of a rough draft is to give you a place to start to put together your ideas with evidence formally. Additionally, writing a rough draft lets you gauge if you need to do more research, [or] change purpose...."[22]

To complete a rough draft, students will be assigned a "chunk" of the final paper to be submitted before the final draft. Of course, each professor is different, but you can expect the rough draft to be anywhere from ten to fifteen pages in length. Primarily, students like to submit the first ten to fifteen pages of their paper; however, some individuals like to write the introduction after the entire paper is complete. That is personal preference, but it can be easier to write this way. If you are one of the select people who write the introduction last, speak with the instructor before submitting the assignment. The instructor will be able to let you know the parameters of the rough draft. The primary purpose of the draft is to get you writing so that your instructor can examine the content of the essay, assuring you that you are indeed on the right track.

Corresponding with the rough draft, many instructors will assign a peer review. Peer reviews are designed to help students become better writers because they allow you to read your peers' work, establishing if the writing style is correct and the content flows. It is arguable that the more you peer review, the better writers you will become. So, take this assignment seriously, but kindly. Your peer has tried his or her best to create an excellent paper; thus, you do not want to be

---

[22] Elftmann Student Center, *A Guide on How To: Write A Rough Draft*, (Minneapolis: Dunwoody College of Technology, 2012), 2.

discouraging. Edit the paper with the saying "we encourage, not discourage," in mind. Tell your peer what needs to be corrected but do it in a way that makes you a hype-man—building each other up as best that you can. Students who support each other are essential to learning; even when you compete, their goal is the same as yours: to get the best grade possible and pass the course. The purpose of a peer review outside of critical writing skills is to help students clarify their point of view or argument while formulating questions about their peers' assignments. Peer review is immensely beneficial to all students as it helps cut back on last-minute drafts revisions, saving you time and effort on grammatical issues.[23]

There is more than one way to complete this assignment. You may exchange papers and check them in class, or you may be assigned a paper through an LMS (learning management system) like Canvas. Peer reviewing through an LMS is simple but ask the instructor or search for a quick tutorial if you are confused. There is an abundance of tutorials available on LMS, so use them. Either way, the assignment goals are still the same.

---

[23] "Benefits of Peer Review." *Southwestern University*, accessed September 13, 2021, https://www.southwestern.edu/offices/writing/faculty-resources-for-writing-instruction/peer-review/benefits-of-peer-review/

3.4 Final Draft of the Research Paper

You are writing the final draft of the Capstone research paper, and this is the version that will be graded most exhaustively. Additionally, you will be presenting the content of this paper to an audience of your peers. There are several things that you can do to improve the grade of your paper.

- **Structure**: The structure of your paper is not the place to get creative; you get creative with the content of your paper. The structure for all academic papers is the same. First, you will have a cover page that includes the title of your paper, course number, the professor's name, and the date. MLA does not require a cover page; however, the instructor may require it for this assignment.

  The title of the paper should be something creative. Do not simply title it "Capstone Final Paper." Come up with a title that makes people want to read it and entice the audience with an exciting statement about the paper.

  The cover page and title are followed by an introduction to the topic, your unique perspective that will add depth to the field, and a strong thesis statement.[24] Next comes the body of the paper; each style of citation offers a slightly different structure for the body of the paper. You can choose to include or omit headings and subheadings, but follow proper style. Finally comes the conclusion of the paper. The summation should mirror your introduction and thesis statement while providing the conclusion you reached through your research. Recall that the thesis statement answers the research question. The body of your paper provides substantial proof that your thesis statement is the correct answer; thus, the conclusion summarizes how you reached the answer.

---

[24] APA requires an abstract.

Remember to refrain from creativity in the structure of your paper. It goes introduction, body, and conclusion; instead, be creative with your words throughout the paper.

- **Perspective:** Always write an academic paper in third person perspective unless otherwise instructed. Third-person perspective reframes from using the word "I." Think about it like this—the person reading your paper, your audience, can assume that it is your opinion without you using the term "I think" because you are writing your interpretations of the information.

- **Grammar/Punctuation:** Grammar and punctuation is an area in which most writers struggle, so ask for help. Go to the writing center at the library, use the computer software available, and read the paper aloud. The writing center can often set you up with a writing tutor to help improve the language of the paper. Modern technology has made editing papers more simplistic. There are programs such as Grammarly that offer free editing app that can be downloaded directly to the computer. This type of app can help with proofreading and plagiarism issues. While the student should be careful to cite and paraphrase properly, at times you may be uncertain if you accurately completed the citation process. The plagiarism checks can help put your mind at ease before submitting the final product.

  Further, take care to avoid the use of contractions. In academic writing, we write that something "is not possible," not that it "isn't possible." First, it is more professional to avoid contractions. Second, it makes your paper a tiny bit longer; you want to take advantage of anything that increases the length of this size paper.

- **Rubric:** A grading rubric accompanies most, if not all, assignments at the collegiate level. The rubric shows how the professor will grade the assignment, and the final paper is no exception. Usually, the rubric for the final capstone paper is extensive, covering essential criteria such as the effectiveness of writing composition, demonstration of discipline depth, effective integration of Liberal Arts education, demonstration of good research practices, and informational presentation.

To earn a good grade on the assignment, the student must demonstrate excellent abilities in all listed areas. The student should examine the contents of the grading rubric, comparing it to his or her finished paper to ensure the named components are appropriately addressed. Additionally, you should refer to the assignment instructions to ensure that all requirements are met.

Once you have reviewed the rubric and the instructions to ensure all requirements are met, the completed project can be submitted. This process does take a little time, and, understandably, it is often omitted from the final review process because you are exhausted from the task at hand. It is advisable to complete the final paper one day and the next day proofread multiple times. The following day, review the rubric and instructions, comparing them against your work before submission. By spreading out the work, you can ward off the fatigue caused by the enormity of the assignment, generating a new focus to finish the assignment correctly.

3.5 Bibliography

The bibliography is the list of sources that you, the researcher, have referenced to learn about, understand, and develop an argument on the topic. The page dedicated to the list is titled differently depending on the citation style. In MLA, the source list is referred to as the Works Cited, APA calls it References, and in Chicago/Turabian, it is described as the bibliography. This section has been titled Bibliography because this text is written in Chicago/Turabian format. Regardless of the title, the list of sources is essential when writing any paper, especially a long research paper. Failure to credit the source for concepts that are not your own is plagiarizing or, stealing another author's work. Speaking from experience, it takes a long time to write an article or book, and the author wants credit for all the hours that he or she logged in creating the document. Plagiarism is a serious offense; as you are aware, it is not worth the trouble. Avoiding a world of trouble is as easy as typing a citation on a bibliography.

Any time you are referencing information that is not your original thought, you must cite where the information originated—giving proper credit to the author who wrote it. In addition to crediting the source, the bibliographic list provides a map to locate the information used to support the central thesis. A bibliography is a valuable tool, as you will learn when I explain source mining in chapter 3. Source mining is when a researcher examines the source's bibliography to identify additional sources.[25]

When creating a bibliographic list, the researcher should save the pathway to any sources applicable to the project as these sources will make up the bibliography list. The purpose of saving

---

[25] See Section 3.4 Helpful Tips and Tricks to Successful Research for additional information on Source Mining.

this information is to revisit the text several times throughout the research and writing process, especially when quoting directly.

In addition to those sources, you have directly referenced either with a direct quote or paraphrasing, you need to list any source you have read to understand the topic at hand. All the information that you have read has helped you conclude your argument. Just because you did not name the source individually within the text does not mean that you are not using the information learned to understand better or explain your analysis.[26] The project instructions will discuss exactly how many sources are required for the assignment; each has a different requirement. However, if the assignment does not have a bibliography listed in the instructions but you reference a source, you must include a bibliographic list to give proper credit.

Moving forward, the arrangement of sources on the source list is generally separated into categories—primary and secondary sources, then subcategories—articles, books, interviews, websites. The categories help the reader understand the various scholarship presented. Aesthetically, it is easier to review the bibliographical list when it is separated into groups.

Unfortunately, when it comes to the creation of bibliographic entries, there is no simple trick. You will need to refer to the style manual to reference how to cite the different sources.

---

[26] "How to Write a Bibliography," *Tippie College of Business: Iowa*, accessed September 10, 2021, https://tippie.uiowa.edu/how-write-bibliography

3.6 Wrapping Up the Major Paper

This chapter has been dedicated to popular writing assignments that you will likely be given while taking Capstone Seminar. While this is an extensive list, it is not exhaustive. Be mindful that other assignments may be issued as well. If you are assigned an alternative assignment, be sure to find reliable examples online to reference.

It is important to remember that good research evolves from a good research question that is answered with the thesis statement. Once you have discovered an exciting topic and developed a decisive research question and thesis, you are well on your way to accomplishing the seemingly impossible.

CHAPTER 4: UNDERSTANDING THE RESEARCH

"For this assignment, students are required to have five (5) primary sources and ten (10) secondary sources." We have all heard a variation of this sentence from an instructor over our educational career. The general assumption is that you understand the differences between a primary and a secondary source and can locate them, and this assumption exacerbates your lack of adequate training. The sad truth is that not all high schools have accessed to inadequately trained staff or resources. While the staff in high schools are trying their very best, if the instructor does not understand how to properly utilize database search engines then it becomes a deficit in the student's ability to research. The digitization of resources can be a blessing or a curse as less information is held in the physical library, and more is available at your fingertips.

This chapter will address primary and secondary sources, including advice about hot to determine the difference, understand source validity, and search effectively. Additionally, database usage will be addressed due to the project demands for peer-reviewed sources. The research process can be pretty enjoyable and understanding various scholarship and locating said scholarship goes a long way in making this an enjoyable experience.

4.1 Primary vs. Secondary Sources

In this section, you will explore the difference between primary and secondary sources. Hands down, this is the most requested review item in any course that requires a significant paper: "please, go over the difference between a primary and secondary source, again." Though I have several theories about why this request occurs multiple times per semester, the leading theory is that students were never properly taught the difference. Perhaps it was because their teachers could not find a method of explaining it that resonated with the student body, or perhaps more accurate, primary and secondary sources can be complicated to tell apart. My theory is irrelevant because students largely struggle with this; you will not benefit from my theoretical ramblings. What you need is a clear understanding of the differences between primary and secondary sources.

Allow me to start with definitions and build from there. These definitions come directly from the University of Massachusetts Boston's Research Guides.

- "**Primary sources** are immediate, first-hand accounts of a topic, from people who had a direct connection with it."

- "**Secondary Sources** are one step removed from primary sources, though they often quote or otherwise use primary sources." [27]

---

[27] "Primary Sources: A Research Guide," *Healey Library at the University of Massachusetts Boston,* accessed July 31, 2021. https://umb.libguides.com/PrimarySources/secondary

Now, I know what you are probably thinking, "yeah, I saw these definitions a million times and I still don't understand the difference." You are not alone!

- **Primary Sources:** When you research a topic, for example the "Aftermath of 9/11," you would find sources from survivors, first responders, and/or newspaper articles from September 11th, 2001, all of which are considered primary sources. Significant confusion occurs with online sources. An entire website is not the primary source; however, documents located on the website can be primary. The medium from which you found the electronic source is irrelevant in terms of ascertaining if it is indeed primary or secondary; instead, it is the date and kind of source that makes it primary. Just because you looked at the Declaration of Independence on the internet does not mean it is a secondary source. It is still a primary source document because it is an imagine of the archived original document.

  Students who study the health sciences struggle with determining the differences between these sources. Many students in this discipline attempt to identify primary sources based on the date alone. They tend to think a primary source must be "old." That is not the case when it comes to medical studies. Think of COVID; the primary sources are being created now. The Pfizer vaccine trials illuminating the vaccine's possible side effects are an example of a primary source.

  When searching for a primary source, you will be advised to visit the campus library or an archive; however, in the digital age, many primary sources are available online. Electric archives are becoming plentiful, which gives us access to a broader range of sources. It is important to remember that what makes a source primary is that it is a first-hand account, not simply because it is "old."

- **Secondary sources** are often easier to locate, and most books on your topic in question are secondary sources. A journal article is an excellent secondary source and one that you will be required to use extensively. These databases house a plethora of peer-reviewed collections of scholarly periodicals or online journal articles.[28]

---

[28] Please refer to sections 4.2 and 4.4 for more detail on online journal articles.

4.2 Knowing the Validity of a Source

Ready for it? Here comes that term that you should be getting tired of—reliability. It is essential to know that the source you have selected is knowledgeable and reliable. Conducting research goes beyond locating the physical source. Once the source is located, you must verify that it is, in fact, reliable. Living in the information age, students are generally good at spotting fake news or a ridiculous article on a topic. Generally, you all know that information found on social media is immediately questionable. That does not mean that it is not reliable; it just means that you need to verify the facts before using it as a reference. This caution should be applied to all research.

Yes, the information found on one of the school's databases is most likely peer-reviewed and written by an expert in his or her field; however, you must examine the author's credibility within that field. For example, an individual's Ph.D. in history does not make that person a credible source on Quantum Physics. Credibility is obtained through experience and education. For the person with a doctoral degree in history to be considered an expert in quantum physics, he or she would need an educational background in the sciences and have extensive working knowledge in the field. Thus, you need to examine the author's background before believing that the source consists of reliable information.

There are a few areas that students should direct their attention to determine the validity of a source.

- **Author:** As a researcher, you wanted to establish the credibility of the source's author. A quick Google search may provide you with all the vital information needed.

  Typically, databases provide peer-reviewed sources, which means that experts in the field [the author's peers] critically review the literature. The literature review checks for factual errors, misconceptions on the topic, or incorrectly used materials, meaning that the author used a source to support the thesis, but the source contradicts rather than supports. This method of review helps scholars produce well-written information.

Perform credibility checks on all sources. Students assume that the author is credible because he or she published book, but this is not always the case. Verify the validity; you spend all day Googling rather silly things, so take a few minutes to Google something important. Moreover, if the author is an expert, now you know to research more work by that author.

It should go without saying that you need to check the validity of all website authors. We all know how easy it is to post blogs and articles on the internet, which means that anyone could get on a "soapbox" to write a bogus article on a topic while appearing to be an authority. Spend additional time researching the internet sources.

- **Date:** Students must use up-to-date information in research papers. Each discipline has a unique frame regarding publication date ranges.

- **Publishing Organization:** If a university publishes a book, then it is most likely a reliable source.

Journal articles tend to be less straightforward. Let us examine the publication of a journal article. A database is a search engine. The database did not publish the article just like Google did not publish a movie; you simply use Google to search for and locate the movie. The publisher of a journal article is the journal, not the database. An example of a journal is the *Wall Street Journal* or *Journal of Economic Literature*. Think of the journal as a magazine that you would see on a shelf near the check out at the grocery store. The magazine prints the articles. Now consider what this means in the digital age. Most likely, you will not see the physical journal [magazine]: instead, it is available online. So, the journal's website houses the original publication of said journal article. You want to verify the credibility of the publishing source.

Websites are even more challenging. Look for education-based websites. Using these, you are more likely to find reliable sources; however, you still need to do the above research to determine if the source is worth using.

4.3 Research Methodology

Research methodology sounds intimidating and complex, but simply put, it is the method you use to conduct research. Research papers habitually have a source requirement, which means that each researcher is required to provide proof of a set number of primary sources in addition to a set number of secondary sources used within the paper. You will be required to have fewer primary than secondary sources. Why is this? Mainly, it is due to ease of access. As with most events, there are fewer spectators than people who have heard about it. Think of this in terms of a fight in high school. We have all been exposed to this type of event. Two people start arguing in the hallway between the first and second periods. There may be ten students nearby who witnessed the fight—these twelve students are primary sources. However, by eighth period everyone in the school knows about the bloody fistfight, even people who stayed home sick that day. In this case, there are significantly more secondary sources on the fight than first-hand accounts. The same goes for the scholarship. There are more secondary accounts because people have conducted research. They have read other's research and their interpretations. In this example, the fight at school is less of a fistfight and more of an argument, but after circulation, the minor altercation turned into a bloody exchange. Therefore, good researchers check the reliability of the source by reviewing the primary source.

Research methodology is the way you collect the sources and the types of sources you intend to locate. When you think of the sources, you probably think primary versus secondary, but it is more micro than that. Instead, think, what kind of primary sources am I looking for? There are diaries, journals, newspapers, legal documents, maps, datasets, and case studies; the list is extensive. For example, suppose you examine an individual's contribution to society, for instance, Steve Jobs' economic influences on the twenty-first century. In that case, you could focus on collecting datasets, newspapers, journals. You are not to collect sources at random, instead collect sources that complement one another. The same goes for secondary sources. What kind of sources are you researching? Journal articles, books, websites, any of these sources carry value if they are pertinent to the central thesis.

Further, the student wants to provide a well-rounded agreement for his or her thesis. That means that you are required to find information that supports the point you are attempting to make and sources that contradict that point. Consider a debate. For example, if the orator only presents information supporting his or her conclusion, the opponent will have a ton of ammunition to present a counter agreement. If the debater considers the supporters and dissenters equally, then he or she will have a stronger argument to stand on, which in turn creates a better dialogue for the spectators.

Research methodology is an essential component of research. The methodology that you use will help guide the central argument of the paper. Students should embrace this term rather than shy away.

4.4 Helpful Tips and Tricks to Successful Research

Another area that students occasionally struggle with is research. We have already discussed how to determine if a source is reliable. Now that we know what to look for, it is time to start looking. Successfully collecting research can be accomplished in many ways. This manual advises you to begin with an internet search, and I prefer to use Google. Many people do not realize how robust the algorithms are on search engines such as Google. An algorithm tailors the results of a keyword search based on the users' chosen links.

While this seems scary because the internet may be watching too much of what we do, it is an excellent asset to research. If you begin your research with a quick Google search, look for academic URLs while skimming the results. You then select a few that might be helpful to your paper. At this point, do another search using the same technique. What you are doing is training Google to pull up scholarly sources for you. Yes, you can use Google Scholar to pull up primarily academic sources; however, the interface of Google Scholar is less user-friendly. As often as students use Google to find information, it makes logical sense to train Google to find the sources you want.

With that being said, on a search engine like Google, you will find articles published on JSTOR, for example, to which you do not have access. There are three ways that a student can go about obtaining access to these articles for free. Do not pay for access to anything until you have exhausted the following options.

1. First, the student should take note that at the bottom of the JSTOR page, there is a link to sign in through "your institution." If you follow that link, it will walk you through the steps to log in. An occasional problem with this method is that the link

will direct you to JSTOR's homepage, at which time you will need to search for the article again.

2. You can open two browsers' windows. The first tab will be the "limited" accessed JSTOR article, then on the second tab, open your institute's library search engine. Copy and paste the title of the article into the library's search bar. Theocratically, the library's search will pull up the article, assuming the institution has to access it.

3. Lastly, assuming you have tried the above options unsuccessfully. You will create an Interlibrary Loan (ILL) request. There will be a link to request an ILL on the school's library page; once the librarian receives your request, the article can be emailed within hours. The ILL is an excellent option tool that students tend to dodge.

Continuing with the institution's library search engine, students must learn to navigate the databases. The databases are selected with the school disciplines in mind. If your school has an extensive nursing department, it will have databases specifically for the health sciences.

There are two ways that these databases can be searched.

1. Use the library's general search engine located on the library's main webpage. This search engine acts as a catch-all for the databases, and it skims through all the available search databases for the key terms entered by the researcher. Now, I cannot speak to the success rate of this method compared to the latter. This method, however, yields an extensive result list, often numbering in the thousands. The search engine allows you to sort and narrow the results into a practical amount.

2. The second option is to search a single database. JSTOR, for example, is a single

database. You can access a single database by browsing the list of databases on the

school's library webpage. In addition to the list of databases, the library provides

descriptions of the collection covered by the database. This description is beneficial

if you are looking for a source specific to a discipline. I will use history for example,

suppose the researcher is looking for a newspaper clipping from the Battle at

Gettysburg during the Civil War. In that case, the research could isolate the

Accessible Archive database, which contains an extensive collection of primary

sources ranging from books, periodicals, dairies, and journals. By isolating an

individual database, the researcher has more control over the types of results

yielded.[29]

Navigating the school's database can be challenging research for many students. When

using the database, think of it as a search engine, like Google. If you want to learn more about the

proper parameters that should be entered to yield the ultimate results, look at the database "User

Manual." As with any manual, it offers a concise explanation of how to utilize the search engine.[30]

Two helpful but somewhat intimidating terms regarding database searches are Boolean

Operators and Truncations. Boolean Operators include the terms—"and," "or" and "not."

Typically, in the advanced search option on a database, the Boolean Operators are located between

---

[29] "About Us," *Accessible Archives*, accessed August 28, 2021, https://www.accessible-archives.com/about-accessible-archives/

[30] "Technical Support," *Accessible Archives,* accessed August 28, 2021, https://www.accessible-archives.com/support/

the blank keyword searches. The operators make it so multiple Keyword Search boxes can be filled out to search for "x and y," "x or y," or "x but not y." Do not let the Boolean Operators intimidate you; they are there to help make the 2,000 + search results received shrink down into a manageable number. Similarly, the truncation is a fancy way of saying, "Look for all the different spellings and plurals of "there"; thus, "they're," "their," and "there" would be searched. Refer to the user manual for the appropriate truncation symbol with the selected database as they vary from database to database.[31]

Additionally, mining for sources is the practice of looking through a source's bibliography for the scholarship that would be useful to your paper. This practice is beneficial for several reasons. Say you find an article that supports the central thesis, then most likely, the sources used within the article are also helpful for supporting its thesis. By looking at the sources used within scholarship, you may be able to find texts that would have otherwise been elusive. Additionally, this is an excellent way to locate primary sources, which can often be obscure. This practice can make students nervous as if they are plagiarizing or cheating; however, rest assured that simply finding a source through a bibliography is not plagiarizing if you are using the source to support your ideas and properly giving credit to the author.

Moreover, it is possible to do a cited reference search for a text that is crucial to your paper. As the Cummings Institute's website "Writing: Literature Reviews for Culminating Project" states, "make like Hansel and Gretel … follow the resource breadcrumbs." The fable is an excellent analogy because a bibliography works as a trail of breadcrumbs. If you follow the trail, it should show you exactly where the information has been used. By completing a cited reference search,

---

[31] "Top Ten Database Search Tips," *Berkeley City College*, last modified April 4, 2011. https://www.berkeleycitycollege.edu/library/2011/04/04/databasesearchtips/

you are looking for the articles in which the critical source has been referenced. In theory, this search should provide you with sources that are written on the topic of interest. To use the search by cited reference option, you will have to hunt for it in the navigation toolbar. Do not be afraid to check everywhere. When in doubt, you can do a quick internet source to ascertain whether the database offers the cited reference search option.[32]

Several problems must be considered before using the cited reference search function.

1. Each database has its unique collection of sources on a particular subject. To ensure the best results, locate the database that houses sources similar in nature to your research. Even if the database covers the indicated topic, it is still possible for the search to yield no results. The lack of results does not mean that the reference has not to be cited within other texts. It simply means that the database's index does not include the text that may use the reference. Be mindful that this search option works best when searching for a citation within a journal article.

2. Another potential challenge of database collection is that each database index is entered differently, so be sure to search all the permutations of the citation.

3. Likewise, if the citation you search for has several authors, the database may only have indexed the first author listed. To combat this complication, try searching for the citation in different formats. The true challenge is that index entries on databases are edited minimally; thus, a spelling or typographical error may be missed. The error will cause future complications for the researcher.

---

[32] "Writing: Literature Reviews for Culminating Project," *CORE: Cummings Online Resource,* last modified October 7, 2019, https://azhin.org/c.php?g=457546&p=3140735

4. If you have tried all the above-suggested search strategies without success, consider the resource's date. It is possible that if the source is too new, then it has not been referenced in publications.[33]

---

[33] Ibid.

4.5 Reviewing the Research

Understanding the differences between primary and secondary sources is a critical skill required to complete Capstone Seminar. Hopefully, this section has served as a great review since many of you understand the differences. Examining the period in which the "event" took place before searching for these resources will help you determine quickly whether a source is a primary or secondary. Moreover, verifying source validity is crucial to producing a well-sourced academic paper. Without reliable sources, the thesis of the work will lack evidence. So, find solid and reliable sources so that your argument is stable. You can collect robust, reliable sources by utilizing sound research methodology.

Researching reliable academic resources can be a challenge; however, the strategies reviewed in this section will help you overcome a lot of your upcoming research challenges.

CHAPTER 5: PRESENTATIONS

The art of public speaking can be a frightening experience for many people. One of the most important things you can do to calm your nerves is prepare. In this selection, I will discuss good preparation and presentation strategies.

You should have completed several public speaking assignments; however, the stress that the Capstone presentation places on students is immense. Think about it; you must complete this course to graduate. You have spent at least four years of your life working towards graduation. Now that you have completed a significant research paper, which in many cases is the largest, most extensive research project that you have complete to date, you must successfully present this information to an audience of your peers in a multimedia presents or posterboard presentation. It can be uncomfortable. Luckily for you, your Capstone professor will give you several opportunities to practice your public speaking skills throughout the semester in the form of journal article discussions.

5.1 Public Speaking Opportunities

Throughout the Capstone course, students will be allowed to present information orally in front of their classmates. A popular assignment is for the student to locate a peer-reviewed journal article and then prepare an oral presentation based on the article's contents. The class will most likely have the opportunity to question the presenting student about the chosen article. This question-and-answer session is an excellent opportunity for both presenter and peer as it encourages social skills and learning engagement. Since the student knows a question will follow the presentation portion of the assignment, he or she will focus on understanding the presented information. Likewise, the presenter is more likely to focus on information that he or she understands in order to be prepared for questions that may be asked.

Before the fear of public speaking kicks in, I encourage you to not think of it as an unpleasant assignment; instead, think of it as a practice opportunity. The wonderful thing about speaking opportunities throughout the semester is that they help build confidence so that you are well prepared when it is time to present the final project.

Following are several good practice tips for engaging in public speaking.

- **Speaking Length:** Learn about the length requirements or expectations before you begin preparing. You certainly do not want to finish short of that requirement. Likewise, you do not want to exceed the time significantly. To prevent either, practice! Keep in mind that you will most likely be nervous when speaking in front of a group— talking more quickly than usual. Be sure to account for nerves.

  It is natural for you to be apprehensive of a public speaking event. According to John Montopoli at the National Social Anxiety Center (NSAC) in San Francisco, "the fear of public speaking is the most common phobia ahead of death, spiders, or heights."

NSAC studies show that 73% of the population suffer from what is known as glossophobia, the fear of public speaking. This fear is classified as a social anxiety disorder, leaving people sweaty, sick, and often with brain freeze.

Several techniques can help reduce the effects of glossophobia, according to the NSAC. First, strive to change how you think about the fear of losing your thought. Do not turn it into a disaster. If you forget what you are saying, it may not be very good at the time, but your audience will forget it as quickly as it happens. Many of your classmates are equally nervous about their turn to present; thus, they will be forgiving because it could happen to them. If a brain freeze does happen, collect your thoughts before moving on. Silence is not necessarily a bad thing when presenting. Often presenters will pause to collect their thoughts before moving on. Many times, the audience does not notice as much as you would assume. Complete perfection is not a genuinely obtainable thing when it comes to presentations. Something inevitably will not go as planned. Unless you have shared your speech with a member of the audience, you will most likely be the only one who knows that you deviated from the original plan. Try your best to be brave and go with the flow. When you relax, you may just enjoy yourself.[34]

Secondly, Montopoli recommends that the public speaker practices his or her speech without attempting to memorize it, asserting that memorizing leads individuals to focus on only one right way of delivery; thus, if you miss a memorized line, it could

---

[34] John Montopoli, "Public Speaking Anxiety and Fear of Brain Freezes," *National Social Anxiety Center*, February 20, 2017, https://nationalsocialanxietycenter.com/2017/02/20/public-speaking-and-fear-of-brain-freezes/

throw the entire presentation off, causing you to freeze. Having brain freeze is a genuine possibility; it happens to the best of us to combat this practice brain freeze recovery from a freeze. To successfully practice recovering from a brain freeze let something distract you while practicing your speech. After pausing for a moment try to pick up where you left off. This practice method will give you the much-needed confidence in knowing that you are prepared to move forward if it happens. Moreover, it is crucial to be prepared for the worst. You can count on something going wrong. While it is not always a significant aspect of the presentation, it may be enough to make you nervous. If you are presenting a multimedia presentation, be prepared to present without it if technical difficulties arise. Good preparation is key to a successful presentation.[35]

The third and final recommendation that the NSAC makes is "learn to relax." When you first appear at the front of the group, your heart may start pounding; you may start sweating or even become shaky. It is essential to take a moment to breathe before speaking. Let yourself accept that all eyes are on you before you start. This moment allows you to slow your heart rate while collecting your thoughts. Then, make eye contact confidently and begin speaking slowly, taking deep breaths as you talk, remembering everyone else is also nervous to present.[36]

As a rule of thumb, if you are prone to nervousness, prepare your presentation to be one to two minutes longer than the assigned time. Creating an extended presentation is done so when you are in front of the group speaking more quickly than expected because the nerves are making you jittery, you will land right around the time frame you had intended. However, nerves could cause you to ramble on and on. You need to

---

[35] Ibid.

[36] Ibid.

make an outline and stick to it. Going significantly over the allotted time is just as bad a being short.

When presenting, a certain level of professionalism will be expected of you, the student. The following points address the conduct that a student should illustrate when speaking publicly.

- **Understand the Topic:** Spend time with the topic that you are presenting. Do some additional research to ensure you understand the topic thoroughly enough to answer any questions you may be asked. Be sure you know how to pronounce names and vocabulary; if you are unsure, there are audio clips on the internet that offer proper pronunciation for just about any word. Then be confident when presenting. Few of the audience members will likely know that you mispronounced a name, so be confident. Knowing and understanding the presentation's content is more critical than the multimedia or posterboard presentation you are preparing. People will remember what you said more than how your PowerPoint slide show looked.

  Equally important to knowing your topic is knowing when to admit ignorance. When speaking publicly, never make up the answer to a question. It is better to say, "I do not know, but allow me to do some research and get back to you," than to invent an answer in front of someone who may know more about your topic.

- **Professional Attire and Posture:** According to the Lumen Education Resources training pages, appearance and posture are vital to a successful speaking engagement. The first impression we have of one another is based on our attire and posture. If you are not dressed appropriately, the audience may be judgmental, causing them to focus on your clothing rather than your words. The attire you select demonstrates a lot about you, such as age, financial status, interests, authority, and confidence level. Now consider the signals that will be sent from sloppy attire. The audience might question your authority to speak on the subject, your credibility, or be so distracted that they may not hear your words.[37]

When you are following the rules of professional dress, you can present yourself in a comfortable well-groomed, appropriately dressed attire. Appearing professionally dressed does not mean that you are required to wear a suit and tie when speaking, but it does mean that a button-down shirt with dress slacks would be significantly more appropriate than cut-off jean shorts and a tie-dyed T-shirt. Understand that your audience is more likely to take you as an authority when dressed in business casual attire, and you will feel more confident dressed in such.[38]

Posture is another important factor of consideration when public speaking. Your audience responds to the kind of posture that you possess. Posture can indicate your confidence level and openness. Speakers can adopt two kinds of posture when speaking—closed posture and open posture. "Closed posture often gives the impression of detachment, disinterest, and hostility."[39] You exhibit closed posture when you stand with your arms crossed or have your hands clasped in front of or behind the body. You can further exhibit closed posture through your attire. If you are wearing a suit jacket, for example, with the buttons closed, that can signal closed posture. Unbuttoning the jacket can make you seem more welcoming.

---

[37] "Appearance: Dress & Posture," Lumen Instructure, accessed September 3, 2021, https://lumen.instructure.com/courses/218897/pages/linkedtext54278

[38] Ibid.

[39] Ibid.

In contrast, an open posture is an inviting, friendly posture that makes you appear approachable. An open posture is accomplished by standing with your feet apart and your head held high. Additionally, having relaxed hands shows an openness to your posture.[40]

- **No Fidgeting:** As a child, you were probably scolded to "stop fidgeting!" it was likely during church, a wedding, or some other significant event where you may have been causing a slight distraction. In children, this is normal behavior that signals nervousness or boredom. Unfortunately, you probably have not grown out of these behaviors as you age, but you can now better control them. You are more aware of fidgeting as an adult because you were corrected for it as a child.

It is vital to bring this behavior once again to your attention as it pertains to the public speaking realm. Students who are nervous about public speaking tend to fidget while speaking. The fidgeting can be a minute action such as wiggling one foot, chewing gum, clicking a pen, or gripping the podium. You are probably not even aware you are doing the action, which is why they have earned the name subconscious fidget. It would be best if you stopped the habit before speaking publicly. There are a few ways to go about eliminating the behavior or, at least, curbing it. Throughout your practice runs, be sure to make yourself aware of the fidgets or ask a friend to watch for them. If the behavior is brought to your attention, then you can focus on eliminating it. Also, try to relax. It is stressful to speak in front of an audience regardless of size, so breathing beforehand may help curb some behavior. Moreover, being well-prepared can give you

---

[40] Ibid.

the confidence you need to help stop nervous behavior. Above all else, keep a positive attitude that you will present successfully and refrain from fidgeting.[41]

When I was in graduate school, I had a lovely professor who had a habit of chewing gum loudly and clicking his pen. I will never forget that class, not because of the fascinating topic Conspiracies in History, but because the fidgeting drove me crazy. I could not focus on my professor's words because all I could hear was the chewing and clicking. It has been eight years since I was in his lecture hall, and I can still hear the sounds. Admittedly, I had a difficult time learning the subject matter because I was distracted. You want your audience to be interested in your words and subject matter. You do not want to be remembered as the fidgety presenter, so be aware of your minute actions.

- **Always have a Backup!** According to Murphy's Law, "if anything can go wrong, it will." I find this statement to never be so accurate as when you are in front of a group of people. Every semester I teach, I jokingly say to them at one point in the semester, "if anything can go wrong, it will in front of 20 people." This ideology needs to be applied to any visual aid that you will be using for a presentation. From the computer and projector not working to the file incorrectly saving to forgetting to bring your flash drive with you, there are one hundred ways that your presentation can go from perfect to marred. To combat this, I insist you always have a backup plan. You should be able to present your content without having a visual aid present. You should have that file saved on a flash drive as well as in a cloud. That way, you have done everything in your power to make the presentation successful in the face of difficulty.

---

[41] Rick Enrico, "How Does Fidgeting Affect Your Professional Presentation?" *Slidegenius* (June 1, 2016) https://www.slidegenius.com/blog/how-does-fidgeting-affect-your-professional-presentation

As an undergraduate, admittedly, I learned this lesson the hard way. It was the final class of my Capstone course, and our professor assigned the presentation order. I was to present first on the last day of class. Public speaking does not bother me. I am not saying it does not make me nervous; I just have learned to manage my nerves. I was excited for my turn to present. It was the very last assignment I was submitting before finishing my degree and off to graduation. Bounding to the front of the room, I inserted my flash drive into the computer only to learn that instead of picking up my flash drive from my computer desk, I picked up my fiancés flash drive. Horror swept over me as I had to admit that I had forgotten my final project and was unprepared in front of 20+ classmates. The instructor told me to "figure it out" in order to present before class was over. All my thoughts now became dedicated to failing the course, not graduating, and realizing all the hard work was for not. Fortunately, thanks to some fantastic friends, I received my project via email before it was my time to present at the very end. I completed the assignment with only minutes left in the class. I would not wish that feeling on anyone, so listen closely. ALWAYS HAVE A BACKUP!

- **Language:** When presenting, you must know your audience and use appropriate language relatable to them. In terms of appropriateness, you want to avoid derogatory remarks or foul language. You do not know what your audience will find offensive, so remain lighthearted and kind. Always err of the side of caution; if there is content that you are questioning the appropriateness of— then exclude it.

  Similarly, avoid using utterances such as "like" or "umm." If you need a moment to think what should come next, simply pause.

5.2 Which is Better—Multimedia or Posterboard Presentation?

As part of the requirements for Capstone, you are required to present your research and conclusions. Depending on the instructor and course requirements, that presentation will likely be accompanied by multimedia, slide show, or posterboard presentation. Each method of presenting is an excellent accompaniment to your oral presentation, and there are, of course, pros and cons regarding each method.

According to the University of Nebraska's 4-H Youth Development Specialist Sandra Stockall,

> "a multimedia presentation is a stand-alone presentation that includes information presented with slides, video, or digital representations and includes sound which might be a narrative, music or sound effects."[42]

[43]

---

[42] Sandra Stockall, "How to Prepare a Multimedia Presentation," *4-H Communications Series: the University of Nebraska,* accessed September 5, 2021, https://4h.unl.edu/documents/Multimedia%20Presentation.pdf

[43] Teemu Pannanen, *Karri Saarinen Presenting at Nordic Design*, (photograph) Stockholm Sweden, September 14, 2017, Unsplash: Photos for Everyone, https://unsplash.com/photos/bzdhc5b3Bxs (accessed September 5, 2021).

A multimedia presentation is a video with which you present the content of your research. Creating a multimedia presentation can be challenging because it requires collecting and creating content, filming, and editing. You must be highly aware of your background, lighting, and noise pollution. Combining the film with the viewing components is an added challenge; however, people are becoming increasingly familiar with the editing processes in the digital age. Free editing software is available online. Generally, applications have free trial periods that students can make use of.

Given that most college students do not have the extra cash lying around to buy expensive software, you will have to be crafty. Search diligently for the free trial periods or free software. While this free software may not have as many available features, it will save you money, and if you use it wisely, it should be enough to get the assignment completed. This type of presentation might be applicable if your class is online. Considering the current COVID pandemic, you should be prepared to present with a multimedia film.

The pros of this type of presentation include avoiding speaking in public. You may have to watch yourself on video, which, admittedly, can be highly uncomfortable, but this method of presenting can make you perform more efficiently because it will eliminate some of the nervousness. Additionally, while the editing process can be complicated, you have the option to edit and re-film. If you make an error, such as brain freeze or dissatisfaction concerning how you said something, you have the option to delete it—simply redo the scene. Editing also allows the student to add content for clarification and impact to benefit the audience's understanding.

On the other hand, the instructor may assign an oral presentation that a slide show must accompany. A slide show presentation is a media form created on PowerPoint, Google Slides, Prezi, or Keynote. The author creates a sequence of pages that include text and images of the content of the topic. This style of presentation is trendy. You may be the most familiar with this method of presenting because it is a standard learning tool that professors use in class. The pros of this method include familiarity, ease of creation, and the ability to include a plethora of visual aids. Since you are familiar with the style of slide shows, students can confidently create and present knowing it "looks" correct. Also, by the time you reach the last year of your colligate education,

---

[44] Charles Deluvio, *Montreal Design Club*, (photograph) Rue de la Gauchetière Ouest, Montreal, QC, Can., December 11, 2019, https://unsplash.com/photos/wn7dOzUh3Rs (accessed September 5, 2021).

you have probably created several slide shows. Your computer probably has all the software available at your fingertips, and there is no scouring the App Store in search of a quality program.

Further, you possibly know how to use the slide show software, which will make the process quick. Lastly, slide shows allow the presenter to embed videos, audio clips, hyperlinks, images, and much more. The options are extensive, which gives you the luxury of designing the slide show to fit the viewing audience best.

On the contrary, the cons of slide shows can be pretty numerous. Occasionally, the creator spends more time making a sophisticated, complex slide show full of animations but forgets that the content is essential. Likewise, the creator may add too much content to each slide. Content overload can distract the viewers, leaving them struggling to read the information and to listen to the accompanying oral presentation. The key to a great slide show is often simplicity, highlighting the essential topics that you intend to cover. The slide show should act as a road map for the presenter and audience to follow throughout the oral presentation.

[45]

---

[45] Jason Leung, *Rise Up with Asians Rally & March,* (photograph) Union Square, San Francisco, CA., Unsplash: Photos for Everyone, https://unsplash.com/photos/2etBbHf3a8E (accessed September 5, 2021.

Another method of presentation is the posterboard. Many schools have a printer that could manufacturer posterboards presentations. Using the printer is an easier option than cutting and gluing the content to the board. The ease of printing allows the student to focus on the content of the presentation. Learning to create a posterboard presentation is a skill that many of us learned in grade school. However, it can be challenging to know what information to include and how to arrange the content precisely. The apparent pro with a posterboard is not relying on technology during deliverance. If you print the posterboard early and remember to bring it with you to class, the posterboard will not cause issues for the presenter (assuming it stands up properly).

On the contrary, you cannot add last-minute additional information to the posterboard, nor can you edit out a mistake. The grammar and editing must be perfect before you print, or you will be forced to fix the error by hand—bringing more attention to the error. Further, you are limited to the kind of visual aids that can be included—printing limits that content to images or text print.

Whatever the method of visual aid assigned with your oral presentation, always focus on the included content. That will allow your visual aid to stand out without overshadowing your words.

5.3 Creating the Visual Aid

Now that you have been assigned a specific type of visual aid to accompany your presentation—you need to know how to make it stand out without overshadowing your oral presentation. Even if you are assigned to create a multimedia presentation, you will still present orally, although it is not live. This section will discuss tips for creating an excellent multimedia presentation, slide show presentation, and posterboard. Be sure to reference this section often when creating your report to ensure accuracy and efficiency.

- **Multimedia Project:** A multimedia presentation may be assigned in place of an in-person presentation. Education is becoming increasingly digital; thus, students need to grasp the elements that make an excellent multimedia present. These presentations are becoming increasingly popular in a business's advertisements, job training, and continuing education. A multimedia presentation is a composite video of slide shows or graphics with a voice-over describing the author's presentation appearing in the video. It is the instructor's preference, but it is highly recommended that you appear in the multimedia presentation. The audience needs to see who is speaking. The growth in popularity is due to the demand for more robust engagement of the audience. By stimulating the auditory and visual senses, it increases the audience's level of focus and retention, making a more significant impact.[46]

  As with any presentation tool, there are potential pitfalls that the user needs to consider. The overuse of audio or visual effects tends to be distracting for audience members. Additionally, there needs to be a good relationship between the color scheme

---

[46] Zahra Hosseini and Anand Kamal, "How to Design Effective Multimedia Presentations," *In 7th International Symposium on Advances in Science and Technology* (2013): 2.

and font size. On the flip side of the coin, the underuse of these effects can leave the audience wanting more. It is a careful balancing act between overuse and underuse to obtain the perfect presentation. Editing is another challenge that you will face. For those of you who are new to the world of editing, editing software can be difficult and frustrating to navigate, so be sure to ask your instructor or a classmate for help when it becomes overwhelming.

According to Zahra Hosseini and Anand Kamal in the article, "How to Design Effective Multimedia Presentations," there are four steps.

1. Plan for your presentation. You already have a topic for the presentation as it will be the same as your research paper. It is not probable or practical to discuss all the research you have gathered within a multimedia presentation. So, you will need to pick the information that you find most interesting. It is highly recommended that you outline to illustrate the most critical information to the presentation and help you organize the information into a logical order. Another consideration is to be aware of the audience members. To whom are you presenting? What is their knowledge on the topic? You want to keep the content informative and exciting to the audience at large, regardless of their knowledge. For example, if you speak about a health science topic in a classroom full of health science majors, then technical terms are recommended. However, if you are speaking on that same topic, medical information, in front of a classroom full of English majors, you would want to keep the technical terms to a minimum or define them as you go.[47]

---

[47] Ibid., Hosseini, 3.

Fascinatingly, Hosseini asserts that the presenter should take on the role of teach rather than information intermediary. If students follow this suggestion, they will create a presentation to teach the class about their topic. You should act as if everyone in the room is learning the information for the first time because it is likely that many are. You have done the research becoming an expert on the central topic, at least in the short run. Generally, teachers cover information in class with confidence, attempting to make it enjoyable using different forms of pedagogy to reach their students. Pedagogy is a fancy way of saying teaching method, so lecture, use of technology, media clip and so on is the pedagogy. Create your pedagogy! Pretend to be the teacher while creating the multimedia presentation. What would you like to see? How would you like to learn it? Lastly, ascertain the type of learning experience you want to give to your audience. The more involved the audience is, the more likely they are to absorb the information.[48]

2. Make a setup for the presentation. You will be required to think of how you want to organize and present the information. Determine the most logical progression for the information.

3. Pick the technology that you will use to create the presentation. Using PowerPoint, Prezi, or Google Slides will be essential to creating the slide show portion of the presentation. You will further have to decide how you will record yourself presenting the information. You must consider your surroundings. What is in the background? Are there background noises? How is the lighting?

---

[48] Ibid., Hosseini, 3-4.

All are essential elements to making a clear, effective recording. Be mindful of the slideshow color and font; please see the section below Slideshow for additional information on the best practices when creating a slideshow presentation. Additionally, you want to create a smooth transition between film and slideshow.[49]

4. The final step of preparing a multimedia presentation is practice. Practice the presentation before attempting to film yourself. It will help your mind create a clear path for maneuvering the information. Speak clearly and make eye contact with the camera and do not allow yourself to be distracted by watching yourself on the screen. The audience can tell the difference. Be sure to edit the presentation after it is created. For more information on multimedia challenges and considerations, please see section 4.1.

- **Slide Show:** "The key to success is to make certain your slideshow is a visual aid, not a visual distraction," says the National Conference of State Legislature. Too often, students get carried away with different fonts, graphics, and images—when the key is consistency. It is acceptable to use different bullet points, numbering systems, or text and images on each slide; however, there needs to be consistency in background, colors, and font style. Avoid flashy transitions and sounds; the audience will quickly tire of these distractions. The flow of a speech is as essential as the content. The creator wants to keep his or her audience engaged and captivated. Also, avoid making the slideshow "cute." You want to be taken seriously as an authority on the subject—you are not putting on an entertaining show for your audience. Simple is better for a

---

[49] Ibid., Hosseini, 7.

compelling slideshow. You want to be creative in photographs, but clip art shows a lack of creativity—avoid using it. Go to the internet to find free creative imagery that the audience will find mesmerizing. You want to locate something that will make the audience lean in to hear more about the image.[50]

Equally important is the content the creator selects to add to each slide. This information presented should be the key points or talking points. The text should be limited without the use of punctuation. The speaker should not read from the slide. The slide serves as a road map to follow while the speaker explains the research conducted and the conclusion reached based on the research. Likewise, be sure to make the font or images large enough for the viewers to read. Text that is too small can cause frustration for the viewer, which leads to them focusing on the text rather than the presentation. Limit the number of slides that are created; constantly clicking between slides is distracting. When timing the slide with your presentation, commit to at least one minute per side. You are speaking to the audience; look at them, know your speech without reading it. The slides should be used as a guide to keep your lecture on track, not as a lifeline.[51]

Lastly, do not put all your faith into the technology. If something can go wrong, it usually does in front of a group, so have a backup prepared. Make sure that you can present without the PowerPoint. It takes extra work to be prepared for the unexpected, but it is well worth it when the unexpected happens. Your instructors will not accept

---

[50] "Tips for Making Effective PowerPoint Presentations," *National Conference of State Legislature,* August 8, 2017. https://www.ncsl.org/legislators-staff/legislative-staff/legislative-staff-coordinating-committee/tips-for-making-effective-powerpoint-presentations.aspx

[51] Ibid., "Tips for Making Effective PowerPoint Presentations."

the excuse that the slideshow is not working; thus, you are unprepared to present. They will assert that you should have been prepared to go without.[52]

- **Posterboard:** According to New York University's webpage "How to Create a Research Poster," "research posters summarize information or research concisely and attractively to help publicize it and generate discussion." To accomplish concision and attractiveness, NYU offers a list of suggestions that includes print size, word count, graphic specifications, and layout. Start with a strong title, something that grabs the attention of viewers to draw their interest. A creative title can make the audience more engaged in the project. Be sure to make the text visible from roughly ten feet away. Keep in mind that you are presenting to an audience from the front of the room. If the audience struggles to read the text on the posterboard, they are not paying attention to your speech.[53]

Similarly, keep the word count to a minimum. NYU recommends staying between "300 to 800 words." The goal of the posterboard is to highlight the research content, not attempt a re-write of the project. Highlighting can be done through clear point statements; bullet points or lists are excellent tools to help accomplish this. Regarding the layout, the author wants to be consistent with a straightforward, clean design. Three critical sections should be addressed at this stage of creation—the abstract, accreditation/acknowledgments, and the work cited. Depending on the citation style used for the final paper, you may have already completed an abstract. APA generally

---

[52] Ibid., "Tips for Making Effective PowerPoint Presentations."

[53] "How to Create a Research Poster," *Libraries: New York University,* April 1, 2021, https://guides.nyu.edu/posters. NYU created this lib-guide to help undergraduate students prepare and present strong poster board presentations; since most universities require a posterboard presentation for course work, this lib-guide can generally help students create exceptional presentations.

requires that an abstract accompanies the final paper. If you have not written an abstract yet, you will need one for the poster. An abstract is a summary of the final paper. You will want to include a brief explanation of the thesis and content so that the reader quickly understands the central point of the research. Be sure to include acknowledgment; you are not likely to have agencies funding the research at this stage of your education, but you may have had help from a librarian, classmate, or instructor. Give that individual credit on the poster.

Moreover, you need to give credit to the scholarship that is referenced. The accreditation can be accomplished by including a bibliography, works cited, or reference list. The bibliography will not be exhaustive as the space on the poster is limited. Instead, cite the most important sources that supported the thesis, placing those on the poster itself and have a hardcopy of the exhaustive (complete) bibliographical information used within the paper while presenting. This way, you are prepared for any additional referencing questions and are giving proper credit to those scholars.[54]

Images should be clear and large enough to draw attention. The point of the graphic is to draw focus, so select images and graphics that jump off the poster. These will be talking points when presenting. Also, graphics can slow the reader's speed, giving you time to discuss and explain the image or talking point. Lastly, be sure to acknowledge yourself, the course, and the institution on the poster. As the author, focus on making a posterboard presentation that you are proud of and that is worthy of attention. Pride

---

[54] Ibid., "How to Create a Research Poster."; "Tips and Tricks for Poster Presentations," *Office of Fellowships, Opportunities, & Undergraduate Research: The University of Vermont,* accessed September 5, 2021, https://www.uvm.edu/four/tips-tricks-poster-presentations-0. The University of Vermont's library gives an in-depth explanation on the critical points of posterboard creation.

in your work will help build the confidence needed to exhibit your research and conclusion successfully.[55]

As previously stated, many schools have printers specifically for printing posterboards. Your instructor should have provided you with guidance regarding its location and the best programs to use. If that is not the case, programs like PowerPoint, Canva, and Adobe offer software for creating posterboard layouts. Select the option that suits your needs best to create a poster with the dimensions 24"x36". Now that you have designed a creative, exciting poster, it is time to edit and print. Editing is critical at this point; once the poster is printed, there is no going back. It is advisable to take a day or so after completing the design before editing. This break allows you to rest and recharge so that you may see mistakes that are otherwise overlooked. Also, it would help if you asked someone to proofread for you. Another set of eyes can help catch silly typing mistakes that you are reading over, once you feel confident that a successful editing session occurred, then prints the poster.[56]

---

[55] Ibid., "How to Create a Research Poster."; Ibid., "Tips and Tricks for Poster Presentations."

[56] Ibid., "Tips and Tricks for Poster Presentations."

5.4 Present that Project—What Do I Say?

You have created a visual aid for your project, you have decided on the content you want to include from the research paper— now how do you deliver that information? You have been advised in previous sections not to memorize your speech verbatim, so you probably wonder how to remember what you want to discuss.

Independent international Speaker Coach Elizabeth Van Den Bergh provides tips for speech preparation in her article, "7 Steps to Prepare a Speech in a Surprisingly Short Time." The tools she presents in this article are also the tools she teaches CEOs to deliver the highest quality addresses possible. The seven steps include "identify your purpose, know your audience, add significance, define your clear message, establish your structure, prepare a strong opening and a strong ending, and rehearse."[57]

Let us explore each step further.

1. **Define your Purpose:** What is the purpose of presenting this information? Are you informing your audience? Persuading them to choose a side? Perhaps you are entertaining the audience with an inspirational message.

   Recognize the purpose of your speech and deliver the message appropriately. For a presentation in a Capstone course, you will inform your audience while hopefully be entertaining enough to keep the spectator's attention.

---

[57] Elizabeth Van Den Bergh, "7 Steps to Prepare a Speech in a Surprisingly Short Time," *Elizabeth Van Den Bergh: The Public Speaker Coach,* February 3, 2020. https://speaker.coach/prepare-speech/. Elizabeth Van Den Bergh is a public speak coach who works with multination companies, the European Parliament, entrepreneurs, and businesses teaching the art of elocution. Her teaching philosophy encompasses confidence, content, and connection. She thinks that if an orator can master these skills, he or she can become an excellent presenter.

2. **Know your Audience:** It is critical to know your audience to deliver a speech that they will understand effectively. As previously noted, *[Section 4.1 - Public Speaking Opportunities]*, you need a basic understanding of their background on a topic when presenting to a group. If you are speaking to an informed audience, use terminology relative to the field; however, if your audience is uninformed, you will need to define terms that are not common knowledge and speak in a manner that a general audience is likely to understand. Otherwise, if the presenter speaks above the audience's knowledge base, the audience is likely to get frustrated and ignore the message.

V. D. Bergh recommends the use of an empathy map when creating a speech.

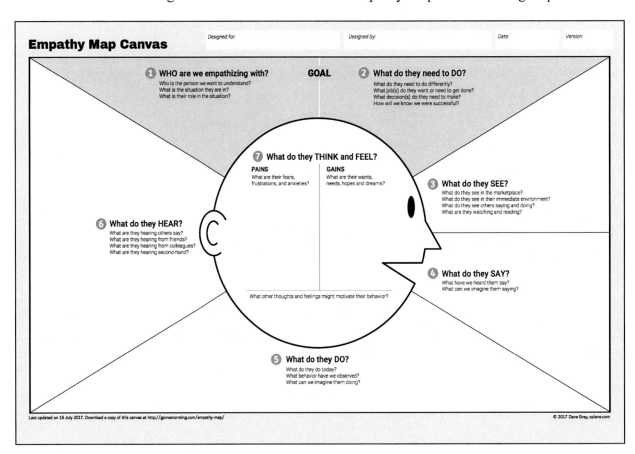

This empathy map template can be located on David J. Bland's blog, "What is an Empathy Map?"[58]

The concept behind the template is for the presenter to look at each area of the map, then add different features to your presentation that will "create your listeners' mental world concerning the topic." The different areas of the empath map incorporate think, feel, hear, see, say, do, pain, and gain.[59]

i.   **Think:** People have their own opinion on a topic, even if they know very little about it. So, consider what people think when they hear your topic. What are any preconceived notions?

ii.   **Feel:** Consider how their personal opinions makes them feel. If you have a "hot button" topic, will it make audience members angry—and so on.

iii. **Hear:** In a world filled with constant media outlets, the odds are that the audience has heard of the topic before. It may have come from the news, the internet, or their peer. Consider whether that information may have been unreliable and plan accordingly.

iv.   **See:** What does the audience see when they think of your topic? Are there advertisements, political campaigns, or billboards that illustrate the concept of your topic that could potentially sway their opinion?

v.   **Say:** When they discuss your topic, what do they have to say? Is it information- or opinion-based?

---

[58] David J. Bland, "What is an Empathy Map?" *Software Engineering Blog: Accenture*, December 21, 2020. https://www.accenture.com/us-en/blogs/bloglandingpage/blogpostpage?wppreview=45257

[59] Ibid., "7 Steps."

     vi.   **Do:** Do they take any action for or against the subject? Do they react?

    vii.   **Pain:** Negatives. Does the audience associate negativity or disadvantages with the subject matter?

   viii.   **Gain:** Positivity. Does the audience feel positivity or see any advantages in the subject?

If you complete the empathy map while planning, it can help during the brainstorming stage. The categories do not need to be organized into any order. Rather it is intended to jog your memory—bring information to the forefront to help develop a way of presenting it.

3. **Significance:** Every speech should have its unique significance. In other words, why is this speech important? Why does anyone care? According to Van Den Bergh, "you win the heart before you win the mind." So, please find a way to win over the hearts of your audience by illustrating how the subject matter relates to them. Van Den Bergh provides an example of Dr. Martin Luther King, Jr.'s speech "I Have a Dream." While King was a very influential Civil Rights activist, he was a successful orator due to this ability to reach out to his audience—making them feel as though the speech was about them. When drafting your speech, channel your inner orator and figure out how to make the audience feel like you are talking about them.[60]

4. **Define a Clear Message**: Making a memorable speech is about limiting the informational overload. The digital age has begun to hardwire us to cram as much information into every moment as possible; however, a good orator will limit the amount of information into one crucial message. The key message should be simplified, no matter how complicated the

---

[60] Ibid., "7 Steps."

subject matter is. The audience will respond to information that they can understand significantly better than an overload of complexity.

To properly accomplish this, the Message House is suggested. This method of simplifying and concentrating a key message is rather popular in the Public Relations field. Below is the image of a Message House. To successfully use this model, the student will create an Umbrella Statement, which is your key message, also known as your thesis statement. Under that thesis statement, the researcher will present three core messages [points] about the thesis statement. Those core messages are supported by evidence, proof points, and support.

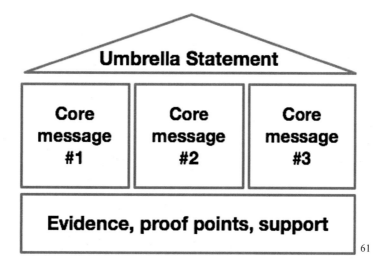

5. **Establish your structure**: To establish the structure of your speech, create an outline. The outline will provide you with the following information, which must pass information to the listener seamlessly. Think of the outline as a roadmap. If you follow it correctly, you will arrive at your destination without getting lost.

6. **Prepare a strong opening and strong ending:** Think back to the last live event you attended; perhaps it was a music concert. Regardless of the genre, all concerts have two

---

[61] Ibid., "7 Steps."

things in common. The musicians have an exciting opening to get the audience pumped up and a radical ending followed by an encore or two. Keep this memory fresh when created a speech. As an orator, you want to open with a memorable story, question, or fact. It gears the audience to want more—the better the opening, the more attentive the audience.

Similarly, the ending should be enthralling. You could close by referencing the beginning, repeating the thesis statement, or motivationally calling action to the subject. Whatever the path you select for the opening and ending of the speech, be sure to think critically about the decision. Mainly, people remember two things from an event—the beginning and end, and it shapes the listeners' experiences.

7. **Rehearse**: To successfully rehearse the speech, you have a few approaches depending on your ability to recall memory. If you do not have a strong memory or are not a "fly by the seat of your pants" person, write the speech out. Once it is written, read it aloud until you feel comfortable with the content and flow, then jump straight to creating a bullet point outline. The outline, as previously discussed, will serve as your road map. As you practice aloud, gradually reduce the number of words on the outline. It is not recommended that you memorize your speech verbatim, and you should know the beginning and end exceptionally well. Learning your speech comes from practice. Practice every chance you get; you will not regret being exceptionally prepared when you are in front of a group of people.[62]

To sum up, speech writing and preparation are all about simplification, knowing your audience, and preparation.

---

[62] Ibid., "7 Steps."

5.5 Wrapping up the Presentation

Making a visual aid or multimedia presentation has many attractive benefits, but if it is done poorly, it can damage your oral presentation's success. Remember that when it comes to a visual aid, the simpler, the better. You are the star of the show when presenting, so do not hide behind the available special effects. Let your visual aid support your authority, not the other way around.

You must present your information in a professional, well-informed manner. By accomplishing this, your audience is more involved, learning more, and you will enjoy talking in front of a group. The Empathy Map and House Message are excellent tools to help develop your research from a long paper to an exciting speech.

The tips for overcoming the nervousness of public speaking are invaluable. The presentation of your research information is an assignment you must complete, so do it to the best of your abilities.

CHAPTER 6: CONCLUSION

The cap-stone to your college education is just at your fingertips. The only thing standing between you and the finale is a capstone project. This text has illustrated how to determine the citation style of your discipline; though, most of you were probably already aware. It has provided you with a review of what citation acronyms stand for, combined with other fields that share your citation format. Do not be afraid to lean on each other throughout the formatting process. It is difficult (no one will tell you otherwise) but the more you practice and the more you read, the better you will become at producing a well-formatted, properly cited paper.

Moreover, this manual has provided detailed elements for creating several of the most popular writing assignments accompanying an extensive research paper. These assignments range from a simple topic proposal to a detailed annotated bibliography. While I hope that the content herein is an enormous review for you, dear well-educated practiced researcher, this manual will provide a concrete foundation for developing the assignments. It is important to note that the proposals, regardless of field, are meant to grab the audience's attention. There is a high likelihood that many of you will write proposals during your career. These proposals may not always be geared towards a major research paper; however, the experience of writing one at this stage will hopefully give you the confidence to tackle the assignment at work successfully. You have the general skills to create a fantastic proposal successfully. While you may not always have the exact specifications of a new proposal type because of this text and the talents you have sharped, learning how to tweak the proposal should be a breeze.

After reading this text, you should have a better understanding of verifying the validity of a source. Scholarly versus popular sources can be tricky to differentiate at times; yet, having the wherewithal to do additional research on the author, publishing company, and source will allow you to ascertain the difference boldly. Furthermore, learning tips and tricks that assist in successfully yielding good search results is a skill that goes far beyond the classroom. Just as learning is a lifelong process, so is research. You will spend much time throughout your life researching the answers to a different question. No, you will not always need to locate a peer-reviewed source, but you will be able to. The researcher will identify the most accurate and best quality sources because of the education received.

Finally, every job has an element of public speaking. It may not always be in front of a room of people, but meetings, briefings, and giving directions to a group are all forms of public speaking. It is a "must-have" skill to be successful in a career. With more virtual meetings these days learning how to create and present a multimedia form of information is incredibly valuable. Yes, this information is vital to the Capstone Project, but understanding that these skills go beyond the classroom helps illustrate this course's value. Plus, begin completely honest, you have spent a lot of money and time working towards putting this cap-stone on the educational experience. It is essential to know that you have developed skills here that will translate into, hopefully, a high-paying, high-reward career. That is the goal of all students. Graduate, get a good job and make lots of money.

The combination of the central chapters of this text house the information you will need to complete the Capstone course with relative ease. While none of the projects are "easy," this manual has neatly organized the information required to complete the project while simultaneously teaching a little more about the research, writing, and presenting processes.

In conclusion, the Capstone project is designed to showcase the research, critical reading, critical analysis, writing, and speaking skills you learned throughout your college experience. While this will be a challenging experience, keep in mind that challenge is good for us, and it helps us grow as intellectuals through the development of our cognitive skills. Face the challenge of the Capstone project head-on, do not let the panic of Wait, How Many Pages? overwhelm you. You will be triumphant now that you have The Bedrock for Conquering Capstone.

BIBLIOGRAPHY

"About Us." *Accessible Archives*. Accessed August 28, 2021. https://www.accessible-archives.com/about-accessible-archives/

"Appearance: Dress & Posture." *Lumen Instructure.* Accessed September 3, 2021. https://lumen.instructure.com/courses/218897/pages/linkedtext54278

"Benefits of Peer Review." *Southwestern University*. Accessed September 13, 2021. https://www.southwestern.edu/offices/writing/faculty-resources-for-writing-instruction/peer-review/benefits-of-peer-review/

"Capstone – BIS," *School of Continuing and Professional Studies: The University of Virginia*, accessed September 9, 2021, https://www.scps.virginia.edu/bachelor-of-liberal-arts/capstone

Chia, Robert. "Peripheral Awareness in Strategic Thinking." *Aes-thesis* 1, no. 2 (2007), 61-7.3

"Citation Style Guides: Home." *LibGuides Mount Aloysius College.* March 30, 2021. https://libguides.mtaloy.edu/citation_style_guides

Cronon, William. "Writing a Research Prospectus." Accessed September 11, 2021. https://www.williamcronon.net/handouts/Writing_A_Research_Prospectus.pdf

Deluvio, Charles. *Montreal Design Club.* (photograph) Rue de la Gauchetière Ouest, Montreal, QC, Can.. December 11, 2019. https://unsplash.com/photos/wn7dOzUh3Rs (accessed September 5, 2021).

Elftmann Student Center, *A Guide on How To: Write A Rough Draft*, (Minneapolis: Dunwoody College of Technology, 2012), 2.

Enrico, Rick. "How Does Fidgeting Affect Your Professional Presentation?" Slidegenius. June 1, 2016. https://www.slidegenius.com/blog/how-does-fidgeting-affect-your-professional-presentation

Hosseini, Zahra and Anand Kamal, "How to Design Effective Multimedia Presentations," *In 7th International Symposium on Advances in Science and Technology* (2013): 1-8.

"How to Create a Research Poster." *Libraries: New York University.* April 1, 2021. https://guides.nyu.edu/posters

"How to Prepare an Annotated Bibliography: The Annotated Bibliography." Cornell University Library. May 5, 2021, https://guides.library.cornell.edu/annotatedbibliography

"How to Write a Bibliography," Tippie College of Business: Iowa, accessed September 10, 2021, https://tippie.uiowa.edu/how-write-bibliography.

"How to Write a Thesis Proposal," *Columbia*, accessed September 11, 2021, https://www.ldeo.columbia.edu/~martins/sen_res/how_to_thesis_proposal.html

"LA 400-Capstone Seminar." *Mount Aloysius College* (2021). http://catalog.mtaloy.edu/preview_course_nopop.php?catoid=1&coid=366

Leung, Jason. *Rise Up with Asians Rally & March.* (photograph) Union Square, San Francisco, CA. Unsplash: Photos for Everyone. https://unsplash.com/photos/2etBbHf3a8E (accessed September 5, 2021).

Pannanen, Teemu. *Karri Saarinen Presenting at Nordic Design.* (photograph) Stockholm Sweden, September 14, 2017, Unsplash: Photos for Everyone. https://unsplash.com/photos/bzdhc5b3Bxs (accessed September 5, 2021).

"Primary Sources: A Research Guide." *Healey Library at the University of Massachusetts Boston.* Accessed on July 31, 2021. https://umb.libguides.com/PrimarySources/secondary

Prospectus Manual. Lynchburg, VA: Liberty University, 2008.

Sheppard, Valerie. *Research Methods for the Social Sciences: An Introduction.* Creative Commons. Accessed June 10, 2021. https://pressbooks.bccampus.ca/jibcresearchmethods/front-matter/preface/

"Selecting a Topic." *Basic Reading and Writing: Lumen.* Accessed September 11, 2021, https://courses.lumenlearning.com/basicreadingandwriting/chapter/outcome-topic-selection/

"Source Analysis." *Basic Reading and Writing: Lumen Learning.* Accessed September 9, 2021, https://courses.lumenlearning.com/suny-basicreadingwriting/chapter/research-tips/

Stockall, Sandra. "How to Prepare a Multimedia Presentation." *4-H Communications Series: University of Nebraska.* Accessed September 5, 2021. https://4h.unl.edu/documents/Multimedia%20Presentation.pdf

"Technical Support." *Accessible Archives.* Accessed August 28, 2021. https://www.accessible-archives.com/support/

"The Importance of Knowing Presentation Content." *Universal Class.* Accessed September 3, 2021. https://www.universalclass.com/articles/business/the-importance-of-knowing-presentation-content.htm

"Top Ten Database Search Tips." *Berkeley City College*. Last Modified April 4, 2011. https://www.berkeleycitycollege.edu/library/2011/04/04/databasesearchtips/

Van Den Bergh, Elizabeth. "7 Steps to Prepare a Speech in a Surprisingly Short Time." *Elizabeth Van Den Bergh: The Public Speaker Coach.* February 3, 2020. https://speaker.coach/prepare-speech/

"What is a Capstone Project at School, College, or University?" Capstone Writing. Accessed September 9, 2021. https://capstonewriting.com/blog/what-is-capstone-project-definition/

"Writing: Literature Reviews for Culminating Project." *CORE: Cummings Online Resources*. Last Modified October 7, 2019. https://azhin.org/c.php?g=457546&p=3140735